COOKING WITH JOSEPHINE

COOKING

WITH JOSEPHINE

JOSEPHINE ARALDO

Strawberry Hill Press

Strawberry Hill Press
616 44th Avenue
San Francisco, California 94121

Distributed by Stackpole Books
Cameron & Kelker Sts.
Harrisburg, Pa. 17105

Second Printing, December, 1977

Manufactured in the United States of America

Edited by Catherine A. Pearsall

Book design by Carlton Clark Herrick

Library of Congress Cataloging in Publication Data

Araldo, Josephine, 1897-
  Cooking with Josephine.

  Includes index.
  1. Cookery, French.   2. Araldo, Josephine,
1897-   I. Title.
TX719.A69   641.5'944   77-8715
ISBN 0-89407-008-8

for my lover, CHARLES

and Jacqueline, Jack, David, Daniel, Mark *and* Richard

Table of Contents

NOTES ON THE USE OF
JOSEPHINE'S COOKBOOK

Notes on the Use of Josephine's Cookbook

Many terms used in cooking — especially French terms — are defined in the **Culinary Glossary.** Where these terms occur in the recipes, they are printed in bold-face type.

On Measurement

When you are cooking with Josephine, there are several things to keep in mind as they differ from the standard American cookbook.

Tablespoon and *teaspoon* measurements are always *rounded,* rather than level, unless otherwise specified in the recipe. Measurement of *cups* is done in the usual manner, leveling the surface even with the top of the measure.

If you measure a teaspoon, half-teaspoon, etc. of salt into your palm and carefully observe the amount, you will be able to measure quickly, without a spoon, from then on — a great time saver.

On Kitchen Aids

Because there is so much interest these days in kitchen aids, I should note here that I have been using, for many years, the professional model of the Cuisinart. I find it an invaluable addition to my kitchen.

On Wine

I am also partial to the wines of California — in part, perhaps, because I have lived here for more than 50 years — but also because they are excellent and relatively inexpensive. Of course my first love, in champagnes, will always remain Möet et Chandon.

On Abbreviations Used

The following abbreviations have been used throughout the book, both in the lists of ingredients and the instructions for preparation:

tablespoon(s) = tbsp(s)	pound(s) = lb(s)
teaspoon(s) = tsp(s)	ounce(s) = oz
quart(s) = qt(s)	envelope(s) = env(s)
pint(s) = pt(s)	

Metric Conversion Tables

Volume

¼ tsp = 1.25 ml (milliliters)
½ tsp = 2.5 ml
¾ tsp = 3.75 ml
1 tsp = 5 ml
¼ tbsp = 3.75 ml
½ tbsp = 7.5 ml
¾ tbsp = 11.25 ml
1 tbsp = 15 ml

½ pt = 236 ml
1 pt = 473 ml
1 qt = 946.3 ml
1 gal = 3785 ml

¼ cup = 59 ml (milliliters)
$^1/_3$ cup = 78 ml
½ cup = 118 ml
$^2/_3$ cup = 157 ml
¾ cup = 177 ml
1 cup = 236 ml

Fluid Ounces

¼ oz = 7.5 ml
½ oz = 15 ml
¾ oz = 22.5 ml
1 oz = 30 ml

Weight

¼ oz = 7.1 g (grams)
½ oz = 14.17 g
¾ oz = 21.27 g
1 oz = 28.35 g
¼ lb = .113 kg (kilograms)
½ lb = .227 kg
¾ lb = .340 kg
1 lb = .454 kg
2.205 lbs = 1 kg

Temperature

200ºF = 94ºC	325ºF = 164ºC
225ºF = 108ºC	350ºF = 178ºC
250ºF = 122ºC	375ºF = 192ºC
275ºF = 136ºC	400ºF = 206ºC
300ºF = 150ºC	425ºF = 220ºC
	450ºF = 234ºC

The recipes give all temperatures in degrees Fahrenheit (ºF). To convert to degrees Celsius (ºC), subtract 32 and multiply by .56. To change Celsius to Fahrenheit, multiply by 1.8 and add 32.

NOW, MEET JOSEPHINE

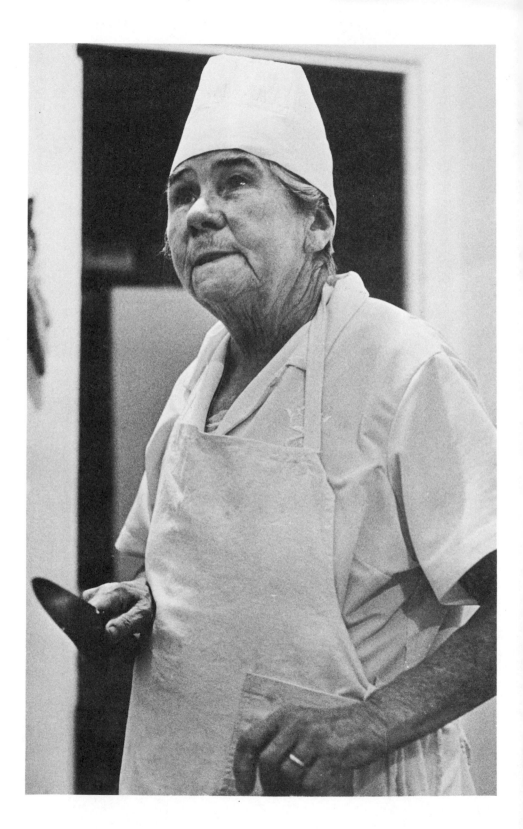

Josephine Enizan was born eighty years ago in the village of Pont-Scorff in Brittany. Her earliest summers were spent tending her grandmother's garden, watching her in the kitchen, and learning from her a love for cooking.

At the age of seventeen, she entered the convent. While there, she decided she could not follow the family profession of tailoring, but would instead become a chef. In Paris, with the help of the Louis Loucheur family (he was at that time a Minister under Clemenceau), Josephine attended the Cordon Bleu for four years. Henri-Paul Pellaprat, legendary chef of the Cordon Bleu, adopted her as his favorite pupil, recognizing her as a natural cook, and often asking her to assist him in class and at his own private dinner parties.

In 1924, on one of their trips to Europe, the Mortimer Fleischhackers of San Francisco dined at the Loucheur's house, met Josephine, and asked if she would come to America and cook for them. Josephine traveled to San Francisco and stayed, working for many prominent families, including the George Oppens, Richard Tobins, Charles Figgenbaums, Isaias Hellmans, and opera singer Lily Pons. Josephine met Charles Araldo in 1925, took the initiative to propose to him, and after a whirlwind courtship of two weeks, they were married.

Josephine returned to Paris many times. In 1927 she again attended the Cordon Bleu, this time for six months, receiving the Diplome in "Les Cours de Cuisine et de Pâtisserie." She began giving private cooking lessons when the society women in San Francisco for whom she worked asked her for instruction. Today she estimates she has taught over 4,000 students the art of French cuisine, stressing the fundamentals and economy, and using her own kitchen as a classroom.

Josephine and Charles live in San Francisco, where she devotes her time to teaching and cooking for the fathers of Notre Dames des Victoires, the church in which she and Charles were married. Her love of life and sense of humor have never diminished, which one realizes in reading the stories she shares in this book as she shares with her students.

**DON'T
LET ANYTHING
DAMPEN YOUR SPIRITS!**

MASTERING THE LEFTOVER

Mastering the Leftover

Knowing how to make profitable use of what is leftover from yesterday's table can be exciting and creative, as well as very useful in keeping food costs to a minimum. Nothing should be wasted in cooking. I learned economy from my grandmother ~ she was tremendously economical. It was her sense of making use of everything that gave originality to her cooking.

The recipes that follow will please the pocketbook as well as the palates of your family and guests. Many leftovers can be prepared as haute cuisine, as canapes, hors d'oeuvres, soups, and entire meals.

On one occasion, while I was working for a San Francisco family, there was unexpected company for dinner. The lady of the house was worried that there was nothing in the house to serve for dinner.

"What do you mean, we have nothing in the house?" I said, "There is a whole leg of lamb left over."

The woman looked horrified. "I can't serve leftovers. It's not done." I promised her I could fix it for her, with breadcrumbs and eight or ten cloves of garlic (which worried her even more). "Let me do it and if they don't like it, I'll fix something on the side just in case." I served the lamb (Restes d'Agneau Sauce Chaplure) and it was wonderful.

I enjoy teaching people to save as they cook. I can teach you something to do with everything besides throw it in the garbage. As my teacher, M. Pellaprat would say, "Any fool can make a roast, but it takes an artist to prepare leftovers so they are palatable and presentable."

While this section deals especially with creative dishes made from leftovers, you will find other recipes throughout the book that also utilize leftovers.

Caprices de Volaille   ## Chicken in Pastry

puff paste (see *Pastry Doughs*)   salt, pepper, nutmeg
leftover roasted or boiled chicken   5 or 6 fresh mushrooms
2 cups heavy **Bechamel Sauce** (see *Sauces*)

Chop chicken very coarsely; sauté chopped mushrooms in a little butter and add to **Bechamel Sauce** with chicken and seasonings. Roll puff paste in a square and cut bands 6 inches long and 4 inches wide; roll ⅛ inch thick. Spread a tablespoon of the chicken filling in the center of a band of paste and wet edges with water. Place another band of paste over the first and seal by pressing edges with a fork. Glaze with one egg mixed with a tablespoon of cream or water. Bake 10 minutes at 400⁰ and reduce over heat to 300⁰ and continue baking for 20 minutes more. *Magnifique et pas cher.*

These may also be deep-fat fried, cooking for a few minutes until browned on both sides.

Cotelettes de Volaille   ## Chicken Cutlets

1 lb leftover roast of poached chicken,   1 cup Sauce Supreme (see *Sauces*)
  lamb, veal or any other meat   ¼ cup heavy cream or
¼ lb mushrooms   concentrated milk
¼ lb ham   salt, pepper, nutmeg
2 eggs   chicken broth

Chop chicken, mushrooms and ham fairly small. Mix with 1 cup of thick Sauce Supreme, salt, pepper, nutmeg, to taste, 2 whole eggs, and cook over low flame until sauce is loosened from side of pan or fairly thick. Pour into a 9" by 13" dish and cool. When cool, take a portion about the size of a large egg and mold with your hands, to form a resemblance of a chop. Roll in flour and sauté in butter or margarine until golden brown. Insert a piece of dry macaroni to imitate a bone and decorate with paper frills. Thin out the Sauce Supreme with chicken broth and a ½ cup of cream. Arrange chops in a circle in a platter coated with sauce, and place a round piece of truffle in center of each chop; serve with sautéed potatoes in center of serving platter.

Restes d'Agneau Sauce Chaplure   ## Leftover Lamb
                                                           ## with Crumb Sauce
                                                           4 to 6 servings

¼ cup butter   6 to 8 cloves of garlic crushed
2 rounded tbsps crumbs   1 to 1½ lbs leftover lamb, cooked
2 to 2½ cups broth   parsley
                                            salt and pepper

Melt the butter in a double boiler. Add the crumbs and stir. Add the warmed broth and stir. Crush the garlic with the palm of the hand or with a knife, and add to the sauce. Cook the sauce in the double boiler for ½ to ¾ hour. Cut the lamb into slices or chunks.

About 10 to 15 minutes before serving, remove the garlic from the sauce, add the lamb, and warm thoroughly. Serve on a warm platter. Sprinkle with parsley.

Variation:
1 tbsp curry powder, mustard or currant jelly may be added to the sauce.

Agneau en Cocotte

Leftover Lamb Casserole
4 servings

2 cups leftover lamb
1 cup bouillon
2 tbsps flour
salt and pepper
1 medium onion, sliced

¼ cup butter or margarine
¼ lb mushrooms, sliced
2 cups grated cheese
¼ tsp mustard, dry or prepared
3 cups mashed potatoes

In a heavy pot, melt butter and add the onion; cook over low heat until the onion becomes translucent but not brown. Add sliced mushrooms, stirring for five minutes. Add flour, salt, pepper, and mustard. Blend gradually, adding the stock or bouillon, and cook over low heat stirring constantly until thickened. Add the lamb and mix well. Turn into a 2-quart casserole and cover with potatoes and cheese. Make crisscross design on top with fork. Bake in 350⁰ oven for 30 minutes until the potatoes are lightly browned.

Emince de Mouton Bretonne

Minced Leftover Lamb,
Brittany style

4 onions
1 clove garlic
chopped parsley
¼ cup butter or margarine

salt and pepper
½ cup white wine
1 tbsp flour mixed in ½ cup broth
leftover lamb

Sauté chopped onions and garlic in the butter or margarine, very slowly until translucent but not brown. Add the flour and warm broth and stir. Add wine, salt and pepper, and allow to cook in a double boiler for about 15 minutes (if too thick, add a little more broth). Cut lamb into small slices or chunks and add to the sauce and warm through. Arrange on a serving dish and garnish with parsley.

Chou Farci — Sauce Brune aux Capres

Stuffed Cabbage with Brown Caper Sauce
6 servings

1 medium head cabbage
¾ lb ground pork
¾ lb lean ground beef
½ lb leftover (cooked) chicken, chopped fine
1 egg
4 scallions, chopped fine, or 2 shallots
1 sprig fresh thyme, leaves chopped fine
3 to 4 slices stale bread
¼ cup broth

1 to 2 cloves garlic, minced
2 pinches allspice, salt, pepper
4 strips bacon
2 to 3 tbsps butter or margarine
Sauce:
4 tbsps butter or margarine
⅓ cup flour
1¼ cups chicken or beef broth
¼ cup **glace de viande**
1 oz capers and their juice
salt and pepper
½ onion, chopped fine

Blanch cabbage leaves for 7 minutes. Generously grease a rounded-bottom casserole with a tablespoon or so of butter or margarine. Lay the strips of bacon criss-crossed with the ends overlapping the rim of the bowl; set aside. Sauté the scallions and thyme in 1-2 tablespoons melted butter, then combine them with the meats, bread (soaked in the broth), and egg. Season with the allspice, salt, pepper and minced garlic. To check seasonings, sauté a small amount of mixture in some fat until cooked through — correct seasonings if necessary.

To assemble: line bowl with cabbage leaves. Pack some of the meat mixture into the bowl. Season with salt and pepper. Lay some more cabbage leaves over the meat and again pack some meat mixture into the bowl. Season with salt and pepper and continue process until all the meat is used. End with cabbage leaves and fold bacon ends over the top. If desired, you can also give a generous splash of brandy. Seal with heavy tin foil, and place in a **bain marie** (pan with water). Bake in a preheated 300⁰ oven for 1½ hours. Remove foil and bake another 30 minutes or until it feels firm to the touch.

Sauce: Prepare a **roux** by melting 4 tablespoons butter in heavy-bottomed pan. Sauté onion and add flour, and brown until it turns very dark. Slowly add the broth, stirring constantly. Cover and cook 20-25 minutes over low heat. Before serving, add the **glace de viande** and capers. Check seasonings.

To serve: Invert dish on a heated platter. Drain off liquid and stir into the sauce.

Ragout de Dinde

Ragout of Turkey

leftover turkey, diced
½ lb sweetbreads
¼ lb mushrooms
½ tbsp each: parsley, tarragon
¼ lb fresh bacon
6 artichokes bottoms (optional)

5 or 6 small onions
salt and pepper to taste
1 tsp curry powder
2 cups white wine or
  ½ wine - ½ bouillon

Soak sweetbreads in cold water for 1 hour; then cover in cold water and bring to a boil and cook 5 minutes. Take out and plunge in cold water. Remove all skin and fat, cut into slices and put aside. Boil the fresh bacon for 10 minutes and cut into **lardons**. Peel and wash mushrooms; peel onions; chop fines herbs.

Dice bacon and fry in a little oil, adding the sweetbreads, the herbs, onion, and mushrooms, and cook for about 10 minutes. Add the wine (or ½ wine - ½ bouillon), salt and pepper to taste, and curry. Simmer for 30 minutes, and just before serving, add the turkey and warm through.

Cook optional artichoke bottoms in lemon water for about 15 to 20 minutes. Arrange turkey on a warm serving platter surrounded by the artichokes, and cover with sauce; sprinkle with parsley.

A purée of yams can be served separately. This dish is classified as "cuisine bourgeoise."

La Potée Nancéenne

Pork and Vegetable Casserole

1 lb pork, diced; leftover meat may
  be used including goose or duck
chicken fat for browning
½ tsp salt
1 small onion
2 to 3 ribs celery

½ green pepper
pepper, thyme and bay leaf
2 cups cooked rice
2 cups sauerkraut or cabbage
2 tbsps butter

Cook the rice.

Brown pork and chopped vegetables in chicken fat. Cover and cook slowly over reduced heat until well-cooked. Season with salt, pepper and herbs. In a filmed casserole make layers of cooked rice, pork and vegetables, and sauerkraut with its juice. Dot with butter and cover casserole. Bake for 45 minutes at 350°.

Tourton Edith

Meat Turnover
4 servings

1 recipe pâte brisée (see *Pastry Dough*)
3 medium potatoes, diced
1 leftover skirt steak, cubed

1 large onion, sliced
salt and pepper
1 white turnip or rutabaga

Preheat oven to 375°.

Roll pâte brisée in a large circle as for a pie, 9 to 10 inches in diameter. On one half of dough put a layer of potatoes, then meat, and finally onions and turnip, each layer being seasoned to taste with salt and pepper. Fold over remaining dough and seal edges with a fork.

Glaze turnover with either oil, butter, cream or eggs mixed with a little milk. Prick with a fork to allow steam to escape and bake in preheated oven for 1 hour.

Desserte de Boeuf Crecy

Leftover Beef in Sour Cream Sauce

1 medium onion
2 cloves garlic
¼ lb butter
2 tbsps flour
1 cup bouillon
½ cup red wine
salt and pepper to taste

1 tsp mustard
1 to 1½ lbs leftover roast beef,
   boiled beef, or pot roast
1 bunch carrots
1 tsp **glace de viande**
½ cup sour cream
parsley

Chop onion and garlic and sauté in butter until golden brown. Add flour and stir until the flour becomes the color of hazelnuts. Add warm bouillon and wine and stir. Cook in a double boiler for 25 to 30 minutes, add mustard, salt and pepper and set aside.

Sauté mushrooms in 2 tablespoons of oil with a chopped clove of garlic and parsley, salt and pepper and set aside. Cut beef in strips ½-inch thick and 5 inches long. Sauté lightly in butter, margarine or oil and add to sauce. Peel and dice carrots; cook in butter 10 to 15 minutes and add to meat. Add mushrooms, **glace de viande** and sour cream. Warm through, but do not boil. Arrange on a warm serving platter, sprinkle with parsley and serve with rice pilaf.

Langue de Boeuf en Mirontors

Leftover Beef Tongue with Onions

leftover beef tongue
3 onions
2 shallots
1 clove garlic
1 tbsp flour
½ cup broth

2 or 3 tomatoes
thyme
bay leaf
marjoram
½ cup white wine
¼ cup butter or margarine

In the butter sauté onions and shallots until translucent; add the flour and warm broth, salt and pepper to taste, wine and herbs. Simmer for about 10 minutes, add tomatoes (crushed), cover and simmer another 10 minutes. Cut tongue in slices, let it warm. Serve on a warm platter, sprinkle with parsley.

Hachis Portugais

Portuguese Hash

leftover boiled or braised beef
   or any other meat
1 onion
½ cup white wine
salt and pepper
2 tbsps oil

butter or bacon drippings
2 or 3 tbsps broth
1 tbsp parsley
2 tbsps butter
1 cup rice
2 cups tomato sauce (see *Sauces*)

Grind meat in meat grinder. Chop onion and fry in fat until translucent; add meat, stir a little and add wine, broth, salt and pepper to taste. Braise in a 350⁰ oven for ½ hour.

Cook rice in two cups of water, add salt and pepper, 2 tablespoons butter; let it come to a boil and simmer for 15 to 17 minutes. Put rice in ring and fill center with the meat and pour over tomato sauce.

Canelons Farcis

Canelloni
6 to 8 servings

Noodle Dough:
  1 egg (for each cup flour)
  1 cup flour

water
⅛ tsp salt
¼ tsp nutmeg

Filling:
  1 lb leftover meat: pork, veal, beef, or chicken (fine chop) *and* ¼ lb. fresh ground pork
  1 onion, chopped fine
  1 clove garlic, minced
  Herbs: thyme, oregano, marjoram, parsley, bay leaf (crumbled)
  grated cheese
  Optional: chopped cooked spinach and/or ½ lb ricotta
  salt, pepper, and oil to sauté meat

Tomato Sauce:
  1 onion, chopped fine
  2 cloves garlic, minced
  1 tbsp flour
  2 lbs fresh tomatoes, skinned, seeded, and chopped *or* 1 qt canned tomato purée
  2 tbsps tomato concentrate (paste)
  Herbs: basil, parsley, oregano, rosemary, bay leaf, marjoram
  4 oz butter and 1 to 2 tbsps olive oil
Béchamel sauce (Optional — see *Sauces*)

Tomato Sauce: Sauté onion and garlic in butter and olive oil. Add flour and cook for a few minutes. Add herbs, except for the basil which is added at the end. Add tomato flavorings and simmer 2-3 hours. (Add the basil at the last minute.)

Noodle Dough: Combine flour, egg, salt, and nutmeg. Add enough water to hold dough. **Fraise** and then let rest 15-20 minutes. This is not a delicate dough; it may be kept in the refrigerator for 1 week, or in the freezer 3 to 5 weeks.

Filling: Prepare filling by sautéing the onions and the garlic in a little oil. Add the meat, salt, pepper, and herbs. Taste to check seasoning. The spinach and ricotta may be added at this time.

Continued

To assemble: Roll and stretch noodle dough as thin as possible. Cut into squares or triangle 5" x 4" wide. Spread filling on dough leaving a space on one end for the bottom. Roll up. Butter a shallow baking dish, 13-15" long, x 9-10" wide, x 3" deep. Line dish with Bechamel or tomato sauce. Lay canelloni side by side in the dish. Pour tomato sauce over all or alternate tomato sauce with Bechamel sauce. Sprinkle grated cheese over all. Bake for 30 minutes in a preheated 375° oven. Check while baking. If it looks too dry, add a cup of broth to moisten. Canelloni may be reheated in a slow oven.

Poisson et Pommes Vinaigrette   Fish and Potato Vinaigrette

about ½ lb or more cooked fish   3 tbsps oil
2 green onions   1 tbsp vinegar
1 tbsp tarragon   1 tsp mustard
1 boiled potato chopped   few drops of Worcestershire sauce
2 fresh tomatoes   salt and pepper
Vinaigrette: 2 hard cooked eggs, stuffed
                                        parsley to garnish

Cut potato and fish in small pieces or dice, season with the Vinaigrette sauce: mix 3 tablespoons of oil, 1 of vinegar, 1 teaspoon of mustard, few drops of Worcestershire sauce, salt and pepper, toss fish and potato in the sauce, add green onion and tarragon chopped. Set on a platter and surround with tomato and stuffed eggs.

Zephirs de Saumon   Puréed Salmon

½ lb salmon, (cooked)   2 tbsps whipped cream
2 egg whites plus 1 yolk   salt, pepper, nutmeg, allspice
4 tbsps heavy cream

Purée salmon in a blender with the egg whites and yolk. It is best to do half at a time. Chill mixture. To add the cream, you will need to keep the mixture chilled. This is best done by placing salmon in a small bowl and setting it in a larger bowl filled with ice. Now add the cream, a little at a time, mixing well with each addition. Add salt, generous amount of pepper, nutmeg, and pinch of allspice.

Preheat oven to 375°.

Film timbales, or any other shape container desired, and fill with mixture. Place in a **bain marie** and cover with buttered waxed paper. Place a cookie sheet across top of timbales or cover container you are using. Bake in a preheated oven for 10-15 minutes. Unmold to serve. Excellent served with **Sauce Colbert** (see *Sauces*).

Restes de Legumes   Leftover Vegetables

All leftover vegetables can be used in soups or salads. For salad, use a vinaigrette or mayonnaise dressing (see *Sauces*). Delicious with strips of ham, cold meat or sausages cut into slices.

Beignets de Gateau   Fritters (Leftover Cake)

stale leftover cake or lady fingers
½ recipe fritter batter:

½ cup flour
2 tbsps sugar
1 tsp cinnamon
1 egg yolk

$1/3$ cup milk
2 egg whites, stiffly beaten
kirsch, sherry, or Cream of
   Maraschino liqueur

To make fritter batter, mix dry ingredients; beat egg into milk, then stir into dry ingredients using a wooden spoon. Fold in the stiffly beaten egg whites.

Dip lady fingers or pieces of cake into kirsch, sherry or Cream of Maraschino liqueur. Coat with fritter batter and fry in deep fat. Sprinkle with powdered sugar before serving. Serve with apricot or custard sauce.

Fromage Pot-Pourri   French Potted Cheese

Grate finely and mix leftover cheeses, including Swiss, Brie, Camembert and any other non-processed cheese. They can be dry. Add a glass of cognac, kirsch, rum, sherry or your favorite liqueur to make the cheese a spreading consistency and put mixture in a covered jar or crock. Keep refrigerated and serve on bread, toast or crackers.

SAUCES

Sauces

Sauces have built the reputation for French cuisine. Therefore, care should be taken in preparing them to maintain the good name of French cooking.

When Mrs. Fleishhacker brought me to this country in 1924, she realized I would be homesick for France. So when we arrived in San Francisco, she said, "Josephine, I am giving you a week off so you can make some acquaintances and meet the French community." After one week I returned and Mrs. Fleishhacker told me she was keeping her cook, Martha, for the day so I might learn how American food was prepared.

I was very interested, expecting to learn quite a bit, for Martha was a good cook. We went into the kitchen where she had prepared a roast of beef, just out of the oven. Martha took the meat out of the pan and proceeded to add flour and water to the pan juices. "Martha," I asked, "What are you doing?" "I am making country gravy," was her reply, and after a few minutes of stirring the sauce, she pronounced it "done."

I didn't say anything, but later Mrs. Fleishhacker asked me, "How did you like Martha? Did you learn something?" I replied, "Martha is a wonderful cook, but no country gravy for me!"

The sauces in this chapter are simple to make because they are derived from definite groups, the fundamental or "Mother" sauces. When you know how to make the fundamentals, you can make innumerable variations.

"La sauce c'est tout." The sauce is everything.

Les Sauces Blanches   The White Sauces

In everyday cooking the White Sauces occupy a much more important place than do the Brown Sauces. The basic white sauces are Sauce Velouté and Sauce Béchamel, and from these two fundamental sauces many others can be made by adding different ingredients. The juices of the dish to be served (fish, poultry, veal, lamb, etc.) are added to the basic sauce to thin it to the proper consistency and to give it the flavor of the dish.

Fundamental Sauce: Sauce Velouté

¼ cup butter
¹/₃ cup flour
1 ½ cups chicken or veal broth
    (fond blanc) — less if juices
    of the dish are to be added.

salt and pepper to taste
nutmeg to taste
1 egg yolk, beaten
¹/₃ cream

Make a white roux by melting the butter in a double boiler or heavy pan over low heat and blending in the flour. *Do not allow it to brown.* Pour in the hot broth and beat until smooth and well blended. (Use less broth if juices of the accompanying dish are to be added later.) Add the seasonings to taste and cook over hot water on very low heat for 45 minutes to 1 hour.

The sauce may be cooled and refrigerated for several days or it may be frozen. When ready to use, heat, adding the egg yolk mixed with the cream at the last moment. *Do not allow the sauce to boil after adding the egg yolk and cream.*

Fundamental Sauce: Sauce Béchamel

This sauce is made in the same way as the Sauce Velouté, but hot milk is substituted for the broth. Use the same method, proportions and cooking time. The juice of the dish to be served may be used for part of the liquid.

Sauce Béchamel and Sauce Velouté are good with poultry, lamb, veal, fish, eggs, and vegetables such as broccoli, cauliflower, asparagus, spinach, Brussel sprouts, and onions.

Derivatives of Béchamel and Velouté Sauces

These sauces can be made from either of the basic sauces, unless otherwise specified in the recipe.

Aurore:

To 1½ cups sauce, add 1 tbsp tomato paste and 1 egg yolk. Serve with chicken, lamb or fish.

Batarde:

Beat ¼ cup butter, 2 egg yolks, ½ cup broth and the juice of 1 lemon into 1½ cups sauce. Salt and pepper to taste.

Caper:

To 1½ cups sauce, add 1 tbsp capers and 2 tbsps white vinegar or white wine. This sauce is good with boiled fish, leg of lamb, and broiled fish.

Chivry:

Add 1 tsp puréed spinach, a little white wine, and chopped herbs: chervil, tarragon, and watercress. Serve with chicken, fish, pork or eggs.

Mornay:

To 1½ cups sauce, add ¾ cup grated cheese and ½ cup white wine. Serve with fish, any meat or vegetable.

Mousseline:

Beat ½ cup butter, ½ cup whipped cream, 3 egg yolks, and the juice of 1 lemon into 1½ cups sauce.

Moutarde:

Add 1 tsp dry mustard to 1½ cups sauce. Recommended with grilled herring.

Nantua:

Add cayenne pepper or 1 tbsp paprika and shrimp butter (chopped shrimps mixed with butter) to 1½ cups sauce. Sauce should be pink in color. Serve with fish.

Normande:

Use some fish stock as part of the liquid in making the basic sauce. Add white wine, oysters and juice, 2 egg yolks, and tarragon. Serve with chicken, white fish or salmon, or poached eggs.

Paprika:

Sauté in ¼ cup butter, 1 large onion chopped, but do not brown. Sprinkle with 2 tbsps paprika, 1 tbsp flour, salt and pepper, and ½ cup white wine. Add the bouquet garni (of thyme and bay leaf) and simmer for 5 to 7 minutes. Add 1½ cups of Velouté sauce. Simmer 5 more minutes, strain and serve.

Ravigote:

Add chervil, tarragon and chives to taste with 1 tbsp mustard, along with a chopped shallot or the white part of a green onion. This sauce can be served cold on vegetables, fish and cold meats.

Riche:

Add chopped truffles or black olives. Good with lobster, fish, lamb, veal, pork, or steak.

Soubise:

To 1½ cups sauce, add 2 to 3 onions which have been puréed. Serve with braised lamb, poached eggs, veal, cabbage, fish, string beans, cauliflower.

Supreme:

Follow Velouté recipe, using one part fish stock to three parts chicken stock, and adding juice of half lemon with the seasonings. Just before serving, mix in two beaten egg yolks mixed with ½ cup heavy cream and 2 tbsps butter. Do not reheat or let the sauce boil after the butter has been added. Makes 2 to 2½ cups.

Villerary:

To 1½ cups sauce, add 2 egg yolks beaten with ⅓ cup cream, a piece of butter (walnut-size) and the juice of 2 to 3 mushrooms, along with several mushrooms. See Sauce Soubise for serving suggestions.

Les Liaisons Faciles   Thickening Agents

If the sauce is too thin, it can be remedied with binding (liaison) or thickening in three ways:

Beurre manie: Mix 1 tbsp flour with 1 tbsp butter and drop into the sauce which is then brought to the boiling point.

Egg Yolk: An egg yolk can be added to a little of the sauce which is then added alowly to the rest of the sauce over a very low heat.

Roux: A roux can be made of equal parts flour and butter and cooked into a paste. A spoonful of this added to the sauce will cause it to thicken.

Les Sauces Brunes   The Brown Sauces

Fundamental Sauce:

Note: The Brown sauces have **glace de viande** (brown beef concentrate) for their base. They are usually used for meat and game.

2 tbsps shortening	3 tsps tomato paste or purée
⅓ cup flour	⅛ tsp pepper
1½ cups brown broth	½ tsp **glace de viande** (see recipe)

Make a *roux* by melting the shortening in a saucepan, adding the flour and stirring over moderately low heat until it has turned a brown color. Add the broth and stir. Then add the tomato paste or purée. Let it come to a boil. Add the pepper and simmer on a very low fire for about 2 hours. This sauce should not be too thick. If it thickens too much while cooking, add a little more broth. Skim off as much of the fat and residue which rises to the surface as possible.

After it has cooked long enough, add the meat extract. Strain the sauce, cool, and keep in a covered jar in the refrigerator for future use. (It will keep at least two weeks.) Make enough so that you won't have to make it each time you prepare a sauce of the same order. Makes about 1½ cups.

Glace de Viande   Concentrated Meat Extract

The glace de viande plays a great part in the flavoring and cooking of soups and sauces. Our ancestors made the extract from a great many ingredients, and compressed it into cubes to use as needed. Today such extravagant preparation may not seem worth it, but commercially prepared meat extract, made mostly of water, cannot compare to the extract that you make yourself. Made in quantity, the glace de viande can be stored in the refrigerator or freezer for several months. Lean beef is preferred for this recipe because it yields more juice than other meats and has a stronger flavor. Use other meats and bones to supplement the beef.

2 lbs lean beef	2 carrots
2 lbs veal neck	2 onions
2 lbs veal bones	2 stalks celery
2 lbs beef bones	1 tsp thyme
1 calf's foot (optional)	2 bay leaves
1 chicken or chicken parts	1 tsp salt per quart of water
any extra bones, roasted in	1 tsp pepper
the oven until well browned,	
then added to the stock to	
give color	

Remove all fat from the meat and bones. Dice meat into big cubes and cover meat and bones with water, 6 to 8 inches above meat. Bring to a boil, skim surface and add all the vegetables and seasonings. Bring to a boil again and simmer for 6 hours. Skim surface from time to time to remove as much of the fat as possible. Strain and press meat to extract the juice, then transfer back to the pot and simmer for 6 more hours, skimming frequently, until the broth reaches the desired consistency. It should coat the back of a spoon. Transfer the stock to a smaller saucepan and reduce heat as the sauce thickens. Pour the extract into jars and store in the refrigerator. It will keep at least a month this way, and longer if it is reboiled every week. Or, freeze in an ice cube tray, cut into cubes, wrap, and store in the freezer. Use as needed; glaze melts quickly when heated.

 HINT:

When making a brown roux, always use a heavy-bottomed pan.

Sauce Bordelaise   *Makes about 2 cups*

1 cup red wine	1 cup beef stock
1 to 2 shallots,	1 tsp **glace de viande**
chopped fine	(beef extract)
4 cloves garlic, minced	4 tbsps butter or margarine
½ tsp aromatic herbs:	2 to 3 tbsps flour
thyme, sage, marjoram	2 tbsps chopped marrow
1 tsp parsley, chopped	juice of 1 lemon

Continued

In a saucepan combine the wine, shallots, garlic, herbs and parsley. Reduce until only ¾ cup is left. Add the beef broth and **glace de viande.** Keep warm.

Meanwhile, melt the butter in the top of a double boiler over medium heat. Let the butter brown slightly before stirring in the flour. Let the mixture cook together until a deep brown color is attained. Slowly add the wine/broth mixture, the marrow, and lemon juice. Cover and cook over low heat for at least 25 minutes.

Thin the sauce with a little more broth before serving. (If the sauce is to be served with meat, use the pan juices to thin the sauce.)

 HINT:

When making a wine sauce, extend the cooking time to prevent an acid taste. If you wish to make a light wine sauce, substitute broth or water for half the amount of wine required.

Fundamental Sauce:

Sauce Tomate
Makes about 1 qt.

¼ cup butter
2 tbsps olive oil
2 cloves garlic, minced
1 large onion, chopped fine
1 tbsp chopped parsley
rosemary, chopped
1 tsp sweet basil or **pesto**

oregano or marjoram, to taste
salt and pepper to taste
1 qt tomato purée (or 5 to 6
    lbs fresh tomatoes, peeled,
    seeded)
1 can tomato paste

In butter and oil sauté together the garlic, onion, and spices. Add the tomato purée and tomato paste. Cook over low heat for two to three hours. Add basil or pesto (basil and oil) when cooking is finished so its flavor will be be preserved.

Variations:
Clove and allspice may be added.

Champignons:
Sauté ¼ lb sliced mushrooms with 2 cloves minced garlic and 1 tsp parsley in 1 tbsp oil and 1 tbsp butter. Salt and pepper to taste and add to Tomato Sauce. Serve with pasta or roast beef.

Sauce Aurore:
Sauté ½ chopped onion in 2 tbsps butter. Add 1 tbsp flour and cook for a minute. Add 2 oz tomato sauce and 1 tbsp tomato paste. Before serving, stir in 4 oz **creme fraiche** or sour cream and heat thoroughly.

Fondue de Tomates

2 tbsps butter	¼ tsp salt
2 large tomatoes, peeled,	⅛ tsp pepper
seeded, and coarsely chopped	(or more, to taste)
1 sprig each oregano and	
thyme, chopped	

Melt butter in a heavy-bottomed saucepan and add the remaining ingredients. Cover and cook slowly over a low flame until the mixture partly evaporates and thickens to a paste.

Refrigerated, the paste will keep a week. It can also be frozen.

Fundamental Sauce   Sauce Hollandaise

4 egg yolks	½ cup butter,
salt and pepper to taste	cut in small pieces
2 tsp lemon juice	

Beat the egg yolks thoroughly with the lemon juice and salt and pepper. Put mixture in the top of a double boiler over hot water (not boiling). Stir the mixture constantly until it starts to thicken slightly. Then add the butter (cut in small pieces) and beat the sauce until it is the consistency of mayonnaise. Up to ¼ cup more butter can be incorporated, if desired, but it is better to have less than risk separating the sauce.

Remove the sauce from the heat. It will keep warm for half an hour on the side of the stove.

Derivatives of Hollandaise:

Arlesienne:
To 1½ cups Hollandaise, add 1 tbsp anchovy paste. Good with fish, eggs, vegetables or broiled steak.

Bearnaise:
Boil ¼ cup vinegar and ¼ cup dry white wine (Chablis or Sauterne) with two chopped shallots, 1 tbsp tarragon, parsley, chives, salt and pepper in the top of a double boiler until the liquid has been reduced to 2 to 3 tbsps. Put over hot (not boiling) water, and add 3 beaten egg yolks and stir until slightly thickened. Beat in ½ cup butter, cut into pieces, and proceed as for Hollandaise. Sauce Bearnaise is good with vegetables, fish, steak, and other broiled meats.

Chantilly:
To 1½ cups Hollandaise, add 2 tbsps whipped cream and 2 tbsps of **fumet** (fish stock) if it is to be served with fish, or 2 tbsps **glace de viande** if it is to be served with meat.

Chivry:
Follow recipe for Chivry Sauce listed under Béchamel and Velouté derivatives.

Choron:
To 1½ cups sauce, add 2 to 4 tbsps hot tomato paste or purée. Serve with eggs and vegetables.

Citron:
Add ½ tsp grated lemon peel and pinch of cayenne pepper to 1½ cups sauce. Serve with fish or veal.

Curry:
Add 1 tbsp curry powder to sauce. Serve with fish, shellfish, eggs, lamb, chicken.

Maltaise:
To 1½ cups sauce, add the juice of a small orange (or about ½ cup) and 1 tbsp grated orange peel. Good with fish, meat, vegetables or eggs.

Mousseline:
Fold into sauce, 2 egg whites stiffly beaten, and pinch of nutmeg. Serve warm with poached salmon, cauliflower, asparagus, or broccoli.

Moutarde:
Make Hollandaise sauce using tarragon vinegar instead of lemon juice, and adding 1 tbsp mustard. Recommended with fish, vegetables, beef, and veal.

Paloise:
To sauce add 1 tbsp mint infusion (or strong mint tea) and 1 tsp chopped fresh mint. Excellent with hot or cold lamb, and other meat or fish.

Valois:
Make Bearnaise variation and add 3 tbsps **glace de viande** and ½ tsp chopped tarragon. Serve with poultry and eggs.

Mayonnaise

2 egg yolks	salt and pepper to taste
1 tbsp mustard	1½ to 2 cups vegetable oil
(dried or prepared)	1 tbsp vinegar

Mix the egg yolks, mustard, and salt and pepper together. Add the oil, little by little at the beginning. As the mayonnaise starts to thicken, the flow of oil can be gradually increased until the amount needed has been absorbed by the egg yolks. Add about 1 tbsp vinegar, according to taste. Stir and put in a closed jar.

Derivatives of Mayonnaise:

Aioli:
Pound 2 to 6 cloves of garlic (using mortar and pestle) and 1 cup mayonnaise little by little while stirring.

Chantilly:

To make a very thick mayonnaise, add lemon juice instead of vinegar, and 3 tbsps whipped cream. Very good with asparagus, cauliflower, artichokes, and white fish. Also good with chicken and veal.

Fines Herbes:

To 1 cup mayonnaise, add 1 tsp mustard, 1 tsp lemon juice, chopped green onion or chives, parsley, capers, tarragon, chervil, basil or dill in equal amounts (½ tsp or to taste). Good served with cold meats, fish, vegetables and eggs.

Mayonnaise Collee:

To 1 cup mayonnaise, add 1 tsp gelatin, dissolved in a little cold water, then melted over hot water and mixed into the mayonnaise. Serve with fish or molded vegetable salads, or as decoration.

Persillade:

To 1 to 2 cups mayonnaise, add 2 cloves finely chopped garlic, 2 tbsps chopped parsley, 1 tbsp mustard, ½ tsp Worcestershire sauce, salt and pepper and vinegar to taste. Serve warm or cold with asparagus, other vegetables, meat or fish.

Remoulade:

To 1 cup mayonnaise, add 1 tsp chopped capers, 1 tsp sour pickles, 1 tsp mustard, one green onion chopped coarse, pepper to taste, and a pinch of cayenne. Good with cold meats and fish.

Sauce Aurore Froide:

To Chantilly Sauce, add 1 tsp mustard and 2 tbsps catsup.

Sauce Creme:

Whip ½ pint whipping cream seasoned with salt and pepper. Add ½ cup oil by droplets, as in making mayonnaise. Add 2 tbsps lemon juice and 1 tbsp chopped chervil. Serve with cold or warm asparagus or other vegetables, meat or fish.

Sauce Verte:

To 1 cup mayonnaise, add 1 tsp puréed spinach and equal amounts of chervil, tarragon, chives and parsley, all finely chopped. (½ tsp finely chopped green onion can be substituted for the chives.)

Tartare:

Follow recipe for Remoulade Sauce, adding 2 hard-cooked egg yolks (strained) and 2 raw yolks.

Vinaigrette

1½ cups olive or vegetable oil
½ cup vinegar
  (wine vinegar preferred)
¾ tsp salt
½ tsp pepper

French Dressing

1 tbsp prepared mustard
  (Dijon)
1 tsp Worcestershire sauce
1 clove garlic, crushed

Continued

Mix all ingredients thoroughly, dropping the crushed clove of garlic into the dressing.

 ## HINTS: Sauces

Mayonnaise: **For sure-fire results in mayonnaise, when mixing the egg yolk and mustard, add a tsp of hot water or hot vinegar before adding the oil gradually. Pour oil slowly until the mixture thickens, then you can add a little more at a time without fear of catastrophe. Do not forget when making a *liaison* (thickening) with egg yolk, it should never boil.**

To bring back a curdled mayonnaise, take another bowl and add 1 tbsp ice water. Add the curdled mayonnaise by the spoonful and stir constantly.

When making mayonnaise, make in quantity, as it will keep for a long time and is always good to have on hand. To keep it longer, add 1 tbsp boiling water when mayonnaise is made, and store in a well-covered jar on the bottom shelf of the refrigerator.

Derivatives of Vinaigrette:

Cottage Cheese:
To 1 cup Vinaigrette, add 3 tbsps cottage cheese, 1 tbsp chopped sweet pickle, and 1 tbsp chopped watercress or parsley. Serve with any kind of fruit or green salad or with cold meats.

Curry:
To 1 cup dressing, add 1 tsp curry and 1 tsp finely chopped shallots (or the white part of a green onion). Serve with cold lamb, chicken salad, vegetables such as cauliflower, broccoli and cabbage.

Raifort:
To 1 cup dressing, add 1 tsp horseradish, 1 tsp mustard, ½ cup chopped parsley and ½ cup broth. Serve with boiled fish, roast beef.

Red Dressing:
To 1 cup dressing add 1 tsp paprika, 3 tbsps tomato catsup and 1 tbsp chili sauce. Serve with avocado, mangoes, grapefruit, artichoke hearts or hearts of palm. Also good with all shellfish.

Roquefort:
Add 2 rounded tsps roquefort or blue cheese and 3 tbsps sour cream to 1 cup dressing. Serve with green salad or Belgian endive.

Sardine:
To 1 cup dressing add 2 generous tbsps mashed sardines (skinless and boneless) and 1½ tsps caraway seed. Serve with fish or shellfish salad.

Vinaigrette Nicoise:
   To 1 cup dressing add 1 tsp of each of the following: chopped green olives, capers, chopped chives, parsley, and chopped gherkins. Serve with cooked cold vegetables, green salad, hot potato salad or cold lamb.

Vinaigrette Chaude:
   Heat 1 cup vinaigrette to the boiling point. Add 2 chopped hard-cooked eggs, 1 tsp chopped parsley, 1 tsp chopped celery leaves, ½ tsp Worcestershire sauce, and 1 tsp dry mustard. Beat well and serve warm. Serve over rice and hot fish.

Vinaigrette au Fenouil:
   To ½ cup dressing, add 1 egg yolk beaten with 4 to 5 tbsps sour cream. Add 1 tbsp finely chopped fresh fennel. Serve with vegetable salad, hard-cooked eggs, poached eggs, and fish.

Beurre Blanc

Butter Sauce with Shallots

Makes about ½ cup.

¼ cup shallots,
   finely chopped
¼ cup white wine

¼ cup white distilled vinegar
   or white wine
½ cup butter, cut in small pieces

   Put the shallots, wine, and vinegar in the top of a double boiler and cook to reduce until the liquid is almost evaporated, with only about 1 tbsp left.
   Over hot water, add one piece of butter at a time to the double boiler, whipping with a whisk until it is totally incorporated before adding the next piece. Repeat until all the butter in incorporated into the sauce.
   Note: The butter should not melt but should be beaten in, otherwise the sauce will have an oily film to it.
   This sauce will keep several weeks. To reheat, melt 1 tbsp butter and add the rest of the sauce slowly, beating constantly.

Derivatives:

Beurre Printanier:
   Made with fresh peas, green asparagus tips, spinach, tarragon and basil. Mix a soup spoon of each — one cup in all — and reduce to a pulp. Add to 2 cups butter. Keep under refrigeration until used. Can be frozen. For canapés.

Anchovy:
   Mix ⅔ cup butter with ⅓ cup anchovy paste, add a little mustard, pepper and a few drops of cognac or whiskey. For canapés.

Colbert:
   Using a whisk or electric beater, mix the juice of 1 lemon, 2 tbsps **glace de viande,** and chopped tarragon into ½ cup butter (softened). Excellent with fish, vegetables, and grillade (grilled foods).

Sauce Marchand de Vin and Variations

The sauce Marchand de Vin and the two following are in the beurre composé category. They are served with steak, liver, hamburger, etc.

Sauce Marchand de Vin

½ cup red Bordeaux wine
½ cup beef broth (or 1 tbsp
  (glace de viande)
1 tbsp shallots (or white
  part of green onions),
  minced

salt and pepper
small pinch of cayenne
½ cup butter, softened
2 tbsps parsley and tarragon,
  minced

Put the wine, broth and shallots in a saucepan. Reduce them until only 1 to 1½ tbsps is left. Cool.

Stir in the softened butter, little by little. Add the salt, pepper, cayenne, and herbs.

Variations:

Sauce Bercy

Same as Marchand de Vin, substituting white wine for the red.

Sauce Bordelaise

Same as Marchand de Vin, with the addition of bone marrow.

Note: These sauces can also be used to enrich other sauces, such as hollandaise, béchamel, according to your taste.

GARNISHES

Garnishes

Les Garnitures

Generally speaking, a garnish is what the name implies. It is used to complete a dish — to make it more attractive as a whole. They can be a single element or several combined but should always be appropriate to the dish being served. The garnitures are classified according to the dish with which served. They are innumerable. Here are only a few.

Garnishes for Butcher Meat

Algerien:
Potato croquettes. Tomatoes rather firm, cut at top, smeared with oil, salt and pepper, and barely cooked in a warm oven as they should hold their shape.

Ambassatrice:
Chicken liver cut in dices, sautéed with mushrooms in a demi-glacé sauce, and arranged in the center of a platter with tournados around.

Argenteuil:
Asparagus spears, rather short (2 inches), blanched for 5 minutes, sautéed in butter. Bind with the juices of the dish to be served, with the addition of an egg yolk and a tsp of cornstarch.

Andalouse:
Sweet red pepper, filled with risotto mixed with demi-glacé sauce. Small eggplant cut in thick slices with a cavity in center. Fill with diced tomatoes that have been sautéed in butter. Arrange on platter with grilled link sausages between.

D'Artois:
A fondu of onions and tomatoes very reduced, mixed with flageolets beans, and used as a base for a roast, or serve in a vegetable dish.

Berrichonne:
Braised cabbage formed in a baba mold (small) and served around the roast, with glacéd onions and chestnut.

Bouquetiere:
Glacéd small carrots, turnip, peas, string beans, sautéed in butter and arranged separately around the dish.

Bourguignone:
Glacéd onions, sautéed mushrooms, lardons (strips of fresh bacon), sautéed.

Bretonne:
Navy beans cooked and sautéed in butter with chopped onions.

Bruxelloise:
Braised endives, potatoes chateau, brussels sprouts, with demi-glacé or madera sauce.

Garnish for Fish and Shell Fish

Admiral:
Sauté mussels and oysters, dip them in Villeroy sauce, bread and fry them, arrange with mushroom caps, truffles.

Cambaceres:
Frog legs, dipped in béchamel, then in slightly beaten eggs and in bread crumbs, then sauté sic (dry). Serve with mushrooms filled with shrimps, bound with Nantua sauce. Taste for seasoning.

Cardinal:
Diced cooked lobster and truffles, bound with Cardinal sauce and lobster butter; serve with another lobster or fish.

Cancalaise:
Oysters, shrimps, mushrooms bound with Normande sauce.

Castellane:
Quenelles of pike, shrimp croquettes, cray fish or jumbo shrimps, and poached oysters bound with the sauce of the fish to be served.

Daumond:
Large mushroom caps grilled and buttered, filled with a ragout of cray fish, chopped mushrooms, truffles, triangles of fried bread, spread around dish.

Dieppoise:
Small shrimps and mussels, strewn around the dish; pour sauce over all.

Doria:
Cucumber in big dices, sautéed in butter. Intersperse with seeded lemon wedges.

Florentine:
Cook spinach dry, season with butter, put a mound in center of platter, fish on top. Sauce Mornay over all.

Nantaise:
1 doz scallops, mushrooms, shrimps, bound in white wine sauce served in scallop shells and arranged around dish.

Nicoise:
Tomatoes sautéed in butter with garlic, black olives, shrimps; top with anchovies all around dish.

Princesse:
Croustades filled with asparagus tips, fish velouté sauce.

Siberienne:
Hard cooked eggs, cut in half. Take yolks out, fill cavity with caviar; cut cucumber 2-inch hollow and fill with chopped shrimp mixed with the yolks. Blend with mayonnaise; serve around cold fish.

Bouquet Garni   Seasonings

Wrap the herbs in a little package of cheese cloth, or reduce to a pulp. Many ingredients can be omitted if you wish. Remove from the sauce or dish before serving.

1

Bay leaf, celery leaves, thyme, parsley, tarragon, cloves.

For: bisques; bouillon; vegetables like tomatoes, celery, carrots; clam juice; vegetable soup; creamed soups; aspics for salads; fish; meat; meat or fish stock; stew, etc.

2

Bay leaf, parsley, sage, marjoram or oregano, rosemary, basil, chervil, savory.

For: roasts; stews; poultry; stuffing for meat; fish; au gratin dishes; spaghetti; macaroni; noodles; meat turnovers; pâtés; meat loaves; hash.

3

Bay leaves, cloves, thyme, rosemary marjoram, chervil, parsley, tarragon.

For: tomato sauce; baked beans; creole dishes; roast and roast gravies; braised meat and tamalé dishes; beans (dried, mexican, or chili).

Spice Parisienne   Parisian Seasoning

2 bay leaves	1 tbsp red pimento
1 tbsp savory (winter	or red pepper
or summer)	1 tbsp coriander
1 tbsp cloves	1 tbsp fennel
1 tbsp mace	1 tbsp cumin
1 tbsp paprika	1 tbsp thyme
1 tbsp marjoram	1 tbsp oregano
1 tbsp cinnamon	1 tbsp sage
½ cup white pepper	3 cups salt*

Grind and mix all ingredients together.* The salt may be added when making the spice or, according to taste when using it. Dry herbs can be used and blended with the rest of the ingredients. The proportion of the various herbs and spices can be increased or diminished if desired.

Use ½ tsp spice parisienne for each ½ lb meat.

PATES, HORS D'OEUVRES, CANAPES

LOUVECIENNES — Pavillon Du Baary - Portique et Frise
par Lecomte

Pâtés, Hors d'Oeuvres, Canapés

Pavillon du Barry in Louveciennes was the country home of the Loucheur family. (Ed. Note: In a very full political career, Louis Loucheur served as Minister of National Reconstruction in 1919 under Clemenceau, signed the Wiesbaden Accords with Rathenau in 1921, and in the years following was appointed to several high cabinet positions.) For five months of the year, they would be in residence at Pavillon du Barry ~ away from their house in Paris and I would be free to do as I wished.

One day I met Arthur, Isadora Duncan's butler, who mentioned to me that she was in need of a cook. I told him I would be glad to help whenever I was not working for the Loucheurs. I had never met Isadora, but I had heard that no one was able to stay with her for very long because she was so temperamental. I agreed to cook for her on occasion at her home at Rue de la Pompe, and I found that I liked her. We got along well together because I was not afraid to talk back to her, and she liked that. For the next four years, whenever the Loucheurs were away from Paris, I cooked for Isadora.

Isadora used to dance in her living room with her children, Deirdre and Patrick. They were beautiful children, and they'd dance one on each side of their mother. They were so graceful, and I could have sat there all day watching the three of them glide about the living room. But, poor dears, they (the children) were drowned in the Seine in the limousine with the chauffeur.

Isadora was the one who introduced me to champagne. One morning I went in to her room to receive orders for the day, and she asked me, "Josephine, wouldn't you like a glass of champagne?" I had never drunk champagne before ~ all I had tasted was cider. In fact, I had to come to America to have wine!

I said, "If I refuse today, I won't see you until tomorrow. If I refuse tomorrow, when will I taste champagne?" So I said yes, and Isadora told Arthur to open a bottle of champagne "for Josephine." Thereafter, whenever she wanted a glass of champagne she would say, "We must open another bottle for Josephine," adding, "J'aime mieux etre battue que de battre la deche, car je ne pourrais plus boire de Moet et Chandon." (I'd rather be whipped than poor because then I could no longer drink Moet and Chandon champagne.)

We became very good friends, and remained close until her tragic death. Somewhere, I still have the scarf she gave me ~ so like the one that caught in the spoke of her auto, killing her.

Pâté Maison Terrine

Country Pâté
Recipe makes 4½ quarts

1½ lbs fresh pork fat
  or **fat back,** ground
2 lbs lean pork, ground
2 lbs pork liver, ground or
  ½ chicken liver - ½ pork liver,
  or all chicken livers
½ lb ground veal
¼ cup butter or margarine
½ cup minced shallot or
  white of scallions
3 cloves garlic, minced
½ cup white wine (optional)
¼ tsps ground cloves
1 **caul** or several strips of
  pork **fat back**

½ cup cognac or brandy
½ cup heavy cream or
  canned milk
juice of 1 lemon
2 eggs
3 tbsps flour (omit if you
  want spreadable pâté)
1 to 2 crumbled bay leaves
fresh chopped parsley
4 tbsps salt
1½ tsps pepper
½ tsps allspice, ground
thyme to taste

Sauté garlic and onion in ¼ cup butter until the onions are soft or glazed but not brown. Add to ground meat which has been placed in a large mixing bowl with the ground liver and remaining ingredients. Sauté a small amount of the mixture to test for seasoning; adjust to own taste. Line a mold with **caul** or cold strips of fat back pork, over-lapping inside the **terrine,** leaving some overhanging the edge to cover the top of pâté when filled. Fill, fold over lining, and cover dish. (Pâté may be layered using long strips of ham, smoked tongue, whole chicken livers or smoked boiled ham rind if desired. Truffles are also optional).

Bake in pan of water in 350⁰ oven for 1 hour, or 300⁰ oven for 1½ hours. Test with knife for doneness — juice should run clear yellow. Pour fat off while still hot. Remove lid, cover with foil and a heavy weight. Cool to room temperature before refrigerating. Unmold when cold and remove excess fat. Pâté will keep 3 weeks to 1 month in the refrigerator. Store in covered crock.

Note: The **caul** or crepine is the membrane enclosing the paunch or belly of the pig. It is boiled and used to line and cover a terrine for pâté. You can obtain the caul from your butcher. As an alternative pâté lining, you can use long strips of fresh pork fat.

Pâté de Foie Josephine

Josephine's Best Liver Pâté

1 lb of fresh pork liver
¾ lb of pork **fat back**
1 onion chopped
2 cloves of garlic
2 eggs
2 tbsps of flour
1 cup of cream
1 cup of milk

1½ tsp salt
¾ tsp pepper
½ tsp allspices
¼ cup of ground cloves
¼ tsp thyme
1 bayleaf
¼ cup cognac (optional)
3 to 4 slices of **fat back,**
  cut ⅛ inch thick or **caul**

Preheat oven to 350⁰.

Grind liver and fat together or ask the butcher to do it. Chop very fine the onion and garlic; mix all together with the eggs, flour, cream, milk and spices. Line a terrine (meatloaf or pyrex dish) with the thin strips of fat back or with the caul to overlap; place pâté mixture in dish with bay leaf on top. Fold over caul or extra fat back strips, cover dish and place in the center of a large pan filled with water to cover dish halfway. Bake in center rack of oven for 1 to 1½ hours. Remove from oven and take off cover, let it cool and when cool, unmold and chill. May be served in slices as first course, luncheon dish or on bread as an appetizer. This mixture can be put through the blender if a finer texture is desired.

Pâté aux Cèpes en croûte   Mushroom Pâté
Province du Berry

Cèpes, commoner in France than in America, are an edible fungus. Mushrooms can be substituted in any recipe calling for cèpes.

1 recipe Pâté Brisée (See Pastry Doughs)	4 oz. butter (chicken or goose fat, drippings from bacon or oil can be substituted)
2 lbs. cèpes or mushrooms	
½ lb. raw ham	
1 tbsp. chopped herbs or parsley: tarragon, chervil, parsley	2 rounded tbsp. flour
2 cloves garlic, minced	$^1/_3$ cup cream
1 medium onion, chopped fine	2 eggs
bay leaf, thyme (sprig)	salt, pepper, nutmeg
	Glace de viande or meat jelly

Put cèpes under the broiler or in the oven to extract all possible water. Remove stems and set aside a few caps. Grind the remaining cèpes, ham, onions, garlic and herbs together until fine. Melt butter or fat and sauté this mixture. Add the flour, cream and spices. The mixture will be quite thick. Remove from the heat and add the eggs and thoroughly mix.

Line a pâté dish with 1/3 of the Pâte Brisée. Lay a slice of the raw ham on it, then a layer of the cèpes mixture. Arrange 1 or 2 caps of the cèpes, then more stuffing, another slice of ham, etc. until the dish is full. Lay the bay leaf and sprig of thyme on top and cover with remaining piece of Pâte Brisée. Make a hole in the center and insert a little piece of foil shaped like a funnel, or you can use a tube from a pastry bag. Bake in a **bain-marie** in a preheated oven (350⁰) for 1 to 1¼ hours.

When finished baking, remove funnel and pour in some **glace de viande** or meat jelly. Serve warm or very cold.

Note: This pâté can also be made by grinding all ingredients together; proceed as above but mold pâté in the caul of the pork or in a double thickness of cheesecloth and bake in a bread-loaf pan covered with tin foil.

Le Pâté de Saint-Omer, Province de L'Artois
Pork Liver Pâté with Plums

This recipe will yield: 3 molds (6″ x 3″ x 2½″) 15 oz each or 2 molds (8½″ x 4½″ x 2½″) 28 oz each.

1 lb pork liver, ground
½ lb pork, ground
½ lb veal, ground
¾ lb **fat back** or kidney fat
½ lb **fat back,**
  cut in small dices
1 large onion, coarsely chopped
2 cloves garlic
1 cup cream
½ cup milk
2 eggs
2 tbsps flour

¾ tsp ground pepper
1½ tsp salt
¼ tsp ground cloves
½ tsp allspices
1 bay leaf
1 tsp chopped thyme (⅛ tsp dried)
¼ cup cognac or brandy,
  (optional)
12 to 15 large fresh or canned
  plums, peeled and stoned
fat back strips, cheese cloth,
  or pork **caul** (preferred)

In an electric blender combine meat, plums, onion, and garlic with the eggs and liquid. Blend mixture well until it is smooth. Add seasonings. Mixture should be a little on the salty side since it is to be served cold. Line the mold with the **fat back,** cheese cloth, or pork **caul** and place a bay leaf on the bottom. Fill the mold and set in a **bain marie** with the water coming half-way up the mold.

Bake in a preheated 350⁰ oven for 1¾ hours. Test for doneness with a small knife which should come out clean when inserted. If not, bake 15 minutes longer.

Pâté de Poulet
Chicken Pâté

½ lb mushrooms, chopped
½ lb onions, chopped
1 clove garlic, minced
¼ cup butter
½ lb leftover chicken
½ lb chicken livers, cooked
½ lb ham, cooked and
  chopped

½ lb chicken or pork fat
1 truffle (optional); olives may be
  substituted for color only
½ cup heavy cream
2 eggs
2 tbsps cognac
juice of 1 lemon
salt and pepper

Preheat oven to 350⁰.

Sauté the mushrooms, onions and garlic in butter. Put them through the finest blade of a meat grinder, along with the chicken, chicken livers, ham, fat and truffle.

Place the cream, eggs, cognac, lemon juice, and seasonings into a blender. Add the ground meat mixture and purée. When smooth, place in a greased casserole and bake in a preheated 325⁰ to 350⁰ oven for 1 hour.

Let the pâté cool and surround with meat jelly or aspic.

D'Artagnan

Cake of Filled Ham Slices

6 to 8 thin slices of ham

First Filling:
8 oz package cream cheese
a little chopped watercress
1 tbsp Dijon mustard
1 tsp Worcestershire sauce
4 ½ ozs of ripe olives, chopped
salt and pepper

Second Filling:
Pâté fois gras
   or
½ lb boiled chicken livers
   blended with 4 tbsps
   soft butter

Third Filling:
7 oz can tuna fish
1 tsp Dijon mustard, rounded
1 tsp curry
1 heaping tbsp finely chopped
   celery and green onions
2 to 3 tsps mayonnaise
pepper

Frosting:
8 oz package cream cheese
1 tsp horseradish
white pepper
slice of soft butter
finely chopped watercress

Coat very thin slices of ham with the first filling, then layer like a sandwich with more ham and the second filling, etc. until there are six to eight layers of ham and fillings.

Frost the loaf with the cream cheese mixture, coating the sides with finely chopped watercress. Decorate with remaining cream cheese mixture in a pastry tube, and serve, sliced.

Colombine de Crevettes

Round Shrimp Cakes

1 cup small bay shrimp,
   coarsely chopped
½ cup small bay shrimp,
   finely chopped
2 cups milk
¾ cups cream of wheat

flour, bread crumbs, egg
   to coat cakes
oil to fry cakes
salt, pepper, nutmeg
Sauce Nantua (See Sauces)
tomato sauce or ketchup
   for color

Cook cream of wheat with the milk and season with salt and pepper. Cool. Prepare sauce.

To prepare cakes: To the coarsely chopped shrimp add 1 to 2 tbsps sauce and a little tomato coloring. Check seasonings. Fill small round hors d'oeuvre tins or use your hands to form round cakes using the cream of wheat mixture. Make an indentation and fill with the shrimp mixture. Cover with more cream of wheat in order to form round cakes. Chill. Before serving, roll cakes in flour, dip in egg, and roll in breadcrumbs. Fry in the oil on both sides. Add the finely chopped shrimp to the remaining sauce and color with the tomato sauce. Serve Sauce Nantua over the shrimp cakes.

Rouleau au Fromage
Cheese Roll
6 to 8 servings

Rouleau:
1 tbsp fine breadcrumbs
1¹/₃ cups milk
¼ cup butter
¹/₃ cup flour
salt, pepper, nutmeg
4 egg yolks
1 tsp sugar
5 egg whites beaten stiffly

Filling:
4 oz Genvais (or Philadelphia
   cream cheese)
4 oz Roquefort, Boursault, Boursin,
   Camembert, Brie or any soft cheese.
   Any other cheese should be grated.
½ tsp chopped chives
½ tsp finely chopped tarragon
fennel
pepper to taste
dash of cayenne or tabasco sauce

Butter a 10 x 15 inch jelly roll pan, line it with waxed paper and butter the paper. In a sauce pan, melt butter and blend in the flour, salt, pepper, and nutmeg. Gradually add warm milk and stir until smooth; cook over a double boiler 7 to 10 minutes, then remove from heat and add the yolks one at a time and the sugar. Beat well, then fold in the stiffly beaten egg whites. Spread the batter evenly in the prepared pan and bake for 15 to 20 minutes in 350⁰ oven, until brown.

On a second piece of waxed paper spread the breadcrumbs evenly; peel paper away from the baked **rouleau** and turn onto the waxed paper. Ingredients for filling should be blended well and spread on top of this. Roll up as for a jelly roll. To serve, cut the **rouleau** in 1-inch slices and pass with a sauce made of sour cream, chives, tarragon, fennel (about 1 tbsp in all), or mix sour cream with red or black caviar.

Mousse au Fromage
Cheese Mousse

¼ lb Roquefort, Camembert, Brie
   or any soft cheese
4 oz of cream cheese
   (commercial or homemade
   "couer a la creme")
1 envelope unflavored
   gelatin
½ cup herbs finely chopped:
   chives, tarragon, chervil,
   parsley, sweet basil

pepper and salt
1 chopped scallion,
   the white part only
1 cup whipped cream
¾ cup white wine
juice of one lemon
2 egg whites, stiffly beaten
1 tbsp cornichons (small sour
   pickles or capers)
1 tbsp pimento, chopped, for color

Soften gelatin in lemon juice, then dissolve in ¾ cup of boiling water. Mash cheese with the cream cheese and add all of the herbs, onion, pepper, and salt if needed, pickles and pimento. Mix well; add gelatin and mix again. Then add the beaten egg whites. Allow to cool until the mixture begins to jell, then fold in the whipped cream and pour the mixture into a slightly greased ring mold or any 5 to 6 cup container. Chill for two hours or more until firm. To unmold, dip in hot water for a few seconds, and turn onto a chilled platter. If in a ring mold, fill the center with a vegetable salad of Russe, cucumbers, asparagus, etc., or fruits de mer salad. Garnish with watercress, lettuce or parsley and sprinkle with nutmeg or paprika. This makes a delicious luncheon dish served with a Pinot-noir or Chablis.

Fromage Boursin   Home-Made Boursin Cheese

8 oz cream cheese
1/3 cup sour cream
1/2 cup whipped cream
4 shallots, minced very fine
1/2 cup chives (or scallions)
   finely chopped
1/2 cup parsley, finely chopped
2 tsp dry thyme
1 clove of garlic, minced
   very fine
salt
fresh ground pepper

In a bowl thoroughly mix all the ingredients with a fork, seasoning to taste. Refrigerate until ready to serve. The cheese can be eaten as soon as it is made, but refrigeration will give it added firmness.

Rillettes de Bretagne   Pork Spread

3 to 5 lbs of pork
   (fresh butt)
1 lb or 2 of fresh fat of pork
   (belly)
1 tbsp of salt
1/2 tsp of pepper
1/4 tsp of cloves
1/4 tsp of nutmeg
1 to 2 cups of water
3 bay leaves
1 onion
3 cloves of garlic (chopped)
3/4 tsp of allspices
1/4 tsp cinnamon
1 tbsp of tarragon
1/4 tsp of thyme

Cut pork and fat into large dices, then brown just the fat very slightly in a heavy skillet. Transfer to a heavy pot, add all the pork and seasoning with 2 cups of water, cover and put in a 200° oven for 5 to 6 hours, stirring frequently to make sure the meat does not stick to the bottom. When the pieces of pork are cooked and lightly brown, strain (reserving the liquid) and mash them almost to a pulp. Test for seasoning, then add half of the fat from the cooking, mix well, and store in small crocks or jars. When cooled, pour a thin layer of fat over each and cover with waxed paper or lid. This will keep in the refrigerator for one to two months. Spread on rye bread or fresh French bread lightly toasted.

Rillettes can be made with beef, goose, (even rabbit, as is the custom in Normandy), but *always* add some pork fat, 1/2 lb to each pound of other meat.

Les Feuilles d'Oignons Farcis   Stuffed Onion Leaves

1 to 2 large onions
leftover meat of any kind:
   veal, pork, beef, chicken
   game, etc.
1 tbsp herbs, a mixture or one
   of the following: thyme,
   parsley, tarragon
1 green onion
½ lb mashed potatoes

1 egg
pinch each of cayenne, cloves,
   and allspice
salt and pepper
slightly beaten egg
breadcrumbs
2 tbsps butter
2 tbsps oil

Boil the onions for 5 minutes, reduce the heat and simmer for 15 minutes more. Drain and let them cool, then separate the layers one by one (it is very easy to do this if the onion is not overcooked). Drain the onion leaves on paper towels. The heart will be too small to be used and may be saved for other purposes.

Prepare the stuffing: put all the meat, herbs, and green onion through a grinder. Mix this with the mashed potatoes, the egg, spices and salt and pepper.

Put a teaspoon of stuffing on each of the leaves and roll each up in the form of a small sausage (sometimes it may require two leaves). Fasten with a piece of toothpick or with thread. They may be prepared ahead of time up to this point. They will keep two days in the refrigerator, covered, or for several months in the freezer.

When ready to use, roll each little sausage in flour first, then in slightly beaten egg (egg whites can be used if they are on hand), then in bread crumbs. Sauté them in butter and oil, turning them over very carefully. Before serving as an appetizer, dip them in melted butter mixed with mustard. Serve on a tray with toothpicks.

They also make a very good entrée (first course). Follow the same procedure for making the stuffed onion leaves. Lay them in an ovenproof dish, cover with tomato sauce, mousseline sauce, Bechamel sauce, etc. Sprinkle with cheese and bake at 375⁰ until the sauce bubbles.

Mille Feuilles au Fromage   Puff Paste Canapés

1 recipe Pâté Feuilletée
   (See Pastry Doughs)
1 cup milk, warmed
1 egg

¼ cup butter
¹/₃ cup flour
¹/₃ cup cheese, dry and grated
nutmeg, salt, pepper

Preheat oven to 400⁰.

Roll puff paste to ⅛″ thickness, and with a knife or pastry wheel, cut 2½ x 2½ squares. Place squares on cookie sheet and bake for 10 minutes. They should rise a little by that time; reduce heat to 300⁰ and bake another 15 to 20 minutes — they should not be too brown. Cool a little, split in half, fill with cheese mixture (see below), and replace top. Spread tops with additional cheese mixture and sprinkle with parmesan cheese. Warm at 450⁰ for 5 minutes and then briefly under the broiler to brown.

Cheese mixture: Over a double boileˡmelt the butter completely, then add the flour. Cook for 5 minutes, adding milk little by little. Cover and cook for at least 15 minutes. Remove from heat and add the cheese, nutmeg, salt and pepper to taste. Add the egg. If too thick, add more milk. Sauce should fall slowly from the spoon.

Canapés Ivoire

3 tbsps butter
2 tbsps flour
²/₃ cup cream
1 cup canned clams, minced
2 tbsps grated cheese
1 small onion

Mushroom and Clam Canapés

2 egg yolks
pinch of cayenne
¼ lb of mushrooms
lemon juice
6 clam or oyster shells
buttered breadcrumbs

Melt the butter in a saucepan. Add the flour and cook for a minute before adding hot cream and then cook until thickened. Add the cup of minced clams (drained), grated cheese, egg yolks, mushrooms, cayenne and lemon juice. Pile into shells, sprinkle with more grated cheese, onion and crumbs, and bake at 400⁰ until brown.

Talmousses aux Epinards   Spinach Squares in Puff Paste

A talmousse always has a cheese base. There are several varieties — spinach a l'ancienne, pastissiere St. Denis, etc.

½ cup thick Bechamel sauce
    (See Sauces)
butter
¹/₃ to ½ cup grated cheese
1 bunch spinach

salt and pepper
nutmeg
1 egg
puff paste (See Pastry Dough)

Preheat oven to 375⁰.

Simmer spinach in a little boiling water — enough to make 1 cup of cooked spinach; squeeze it dry and chop. Add to Bechamel with the cheese, egg and spices. Roll out the puff paste fairly thin and cut into 3″ squares. Put 1 tsp of filling in each square and glaze with egg mixed with a tbsp of water, being sure to coat the edges of the paste. Bring the four corners together like a little package, glaze again and bake on a cookie sheet for 20 to 25 minutes. The spinach will show a little in the corners. Serve warm or cold.

Canapés d'Eglefin Fumé

1 lb of haddock or any other
   smoked fish or left-over fish
¼ cup melted butter
1½ tbsp flour
1 cup cream
½ tsp of dry mustard or
   1 tsp prepared mustard
dash of cayenne

Smoked Haddock Canapés

1 chopped shallot
   or white of green onions
½ tsp Worcestershire sauce
few drops Tabasco sauce
1 egg yolk
12 rounds fried bread
parmesan cheese
1 tbsp chopped chives or parsley

Boil or steam fish for ten minutes; cool. Skin and remove all bones. Melt butter in saucepan, blending in flour, finely chopped shallots, and the warmed cream; cook over a double boiler until thick. Add pepper, and a dash of cayenne pepper. Put fish through a grinder or mash with a fork, and mix in sauce — the mixture should be thick enough to spread on the fried bread. If too thick, add a little cream. Add mustard, Worcestershire sauce, and Tabasco, and egg yolk. Spread on croutons (fried bread), sprinkle with parmesan cheese and put under the broiler for a few seconds.

Canapés de Bengal

3 tbsps finely minced ham
3 tbsps of grated cheese,
   Cheddar or Swiss

Bengal Canapés

3 tbsps chopped Indian chutney
12 round of bread,
   fried in 3 tbsps butter

Mix ham, chutney to a paste and spread thickly on the rounds of bread. Sprinkle generously with cheese and place under the broiler long enough to melt the cheese. Can be prepared in advance.

SOUPS

Soups

My sisters and I were raised in the convent, and when it was time for us to leave, our mother told us we must learn a trade. One of my sisters chose to learn embroidery for the Coiffe de Bretagne (Ed. note: the traditional headdress worn by the women of Brittany.) My other sister chose to follow our mother's profession and become a tailor. I told mother that was not for me. I wanted to learn to cook, to continue with what I had learned from my grandmother.

I began school at the Cordon Bleu, but it was very expensive. In order to stay, I needed to find a job that would pay my expenses. So I went to Sister Secondille, one of the sisters of the Holy Spirit, and asked her to help me. She told me of a job cooking for the Louis Loucheur family.

"But Sister, I can't cook," I said, "I've been at the Cordon Bleu for just a short time. And I imagine the people in those big places expect everything to be dressed like a horse on parade." But Sister called Marthe, the Loucheur's daughter, who came and interviewed me, and told me that if I would come and cook for them, not only could I go to school, but they would pay for it! So I took the position and stayed there four years. That is why I stayed so long at the Cordon Bleu ~ if I had to pay for those four years, I could never have done it.

Of course, I was not the head chef at the Loucheurs; they had a wonderful cook named Eugene. Mr. Loucheur was a very important man in France; amongst other things, he was responsible for re-establishing relations between France and the Vatican. It was a very great occasion when that Concordance was signed, and I remember the Loucheurs gave a grand diplomatic dinner. Aristide Briand and his entire cabinet were there, as well as Monsigneur Cerruti, the Papal Nuncio. Eugene was so happy that day, very excited that Monsigneur Cerruti would be dining there. Now Eugene never took a drink in his life; when he was hot or thirsty he would always ask me to get him a cup of hot bouillon. But on this very special occasion ~ partly because he was a devout Catholic ~ he felt he should have a small glass of wine. He had just a little wine, but it made him so sleepy that he went to sleep right under the kitchen table!

The guests were about to arrive and Madame Loucheur came downstairs to talk to Eugene. I tried to wake him but it was no use. Madame saw him sleeping there under the table and started saying,

"Mon Dieu, mon dieu, who is going to make dinner?" I told her not to worry, that Eugene had everything prepared and I could finish it for him. She went back upstairs to receive her guests and I fixed the dinner. There were two or three kitchen maids to help me, and we got everything ready.

When the dinner was over, Eugene woke up. "Have they arrived yet?" he asked. "Dinner's over, everyone's gone," I told him. "And who made dinner?" When I told him that I had, he said "Good for you". But Madame Loucheur was very upset. She fired Eugene and told him "If Josephine could take the lead, she can keep it always." I felt very sorry and went to Eugene and told him that I wouldn't be staying long at the Loucheurs.

Eugene went to work for Prince Murat, a direct descendant of Napoleon I's sister, Carolyn Bonaparte. He lived at Rue de la Faisanderie, not too far from the Loucheurs. In the meantime, I had met Mrs. Fleishhacker, and she had asked me to be her cook in America. Before I left, Eugene called me and asked if I would like to work with him for Prince Murat. But I was going to America, and Eugene understood and was very happy for me. And the Loucheurs were very kind to me. They gave me five hundred-franc bonds to take with me.

Pot au Feu

Boiled Beef Consommé

3 lbs short ribs of beef
1 lb chuck
salt, pepper
1 bay leaf
thyme

2 to 3 cloves
4 carrots
4 turnips
3 to 4 whites of leeks
1 large onion

If you are lucky enough to have some *fond blanc* (white stock), use it instead of water. If not, you will need the meat with bones added to cold water and brought to a boil. Skim and add seasonings and vegetables. Brown in the oven to give color to the consommé; skim again, and bring to a boil. Simmer very slowly with cover on the pot for 3 to 4 hours. Before serving, skim fat off the surface. Broth should be very clear and amber colored (you can add a little coloring if not). Serve meat with vegetables around it. (*Note:* you can add or subtract ingredients in this recipe. A hen chicken will make a more delicate consommé).

Variations:

Croutes au Pot

Consommé with Croutons

Slice some French bread in very thin slices, dry to a golden brown in the oven, and sprinkle them over the consommé with grated Swiss cheese and chervil.

Consommé Julienne

Cut a few carrots, string beans, celery, and potatoes in long fine strips. Add to consommé and cook for 10 minutes. Serve and sprinkle with tarragon.

Soupe aux Legumes Grandmère

Vegetable Soup

6 to 8 servings

4 cups liquid from
  vegetable preparation
2 tbsps flour (rice flour
  preferred)
enrichment (optional):
  1 egg yolk, cream
cooked, chopped vegetable
  "discard:" broccoli stems,
  cauliflower heart and leaves,
  asparagus stems, etc.

½ cup butter or margarine
1 cup chopped onion
  (one variety or mixed)
1 cup fine noodles
salt, pepper
small piece of butter

This is a soup my grandmother prepared with the liquid left from cooking a vegetable. By cooking the "discards" a little longer, if necessary, then chopping and combining them with the cooking liquid as described in the method

Continued

below, you have an excellent soup.

Melt butter and sauté onion for a few minutes. Add flour, stir, and slowly add a little of the liquid. Stir and slowly add the rest of the liquid. Crush noodles slightly and add to the soup. Check seasonings and cook for 20 minutes. Add cooked, chopped vegetables. Before serving, stir in at least ½ cup cream, remove from fire and stir in egg yolk, and piece of butter.

Soupe Aïgo Ménagère (Provençal)

3 leeks (white part only)
5 cloves of garlic
1 large onion
2 tomatoes (large) seeded, peeled and chopped
a piece of dried orange peel
6 slices of potato (cut thick)
3 qts of **fond blanc** (veal or chicken)

Garlic and Tomato Soup

a small sprig of fennel
a *bouquet garni* (thyme, bay leaf, parsley)
a pinch of saffron
2 tsps of salt
a pinch of pepper
6 small poached eggs
6 thin slices of French bread

Sauté onion and leeks lightly in a little oil. Add tomatoes (seeded, peeled and chopped), the crushed garlic, the fennel, the bouquet garni, the potatoes and the saffron. Pour the broth over, add salt and pepper. Boil fast for 15 minutes. Take potato slices out. Poach eggs in the soup (3 minutes). Drain eggs on a towel. Put the slices of bread in a deep dish. Arrange the slices of potato and eggs on top of bread. Strain soup and pour over all. Sprinkle with chopped parsley.

Soupe à l'Oignon à L'Auvergnate

Onion Soup
6 to 8 servings

2 lbs onions
3 qts beef broth
¼ cup butter
1 cup flour
½ cup sherry
salt, pepper to taste

grated gruyère cheese
paper thin slices of French bread (preferably stale)
1 fireproof 9″ dish, 2″ high

Peel and slice the onions and sauté them in butter until soft and golden brown; add the flour and the hot broth little by little; stir and cook gently for 25 to 30 minutes; add salt, pepper and then the sherry.

Meanwhile butter the dish. Cut the stale bread in paper thin slices and toast them for a few minutes in the oven. Line the dish with the toasted bread, add a layer of cheese, a ladle of the onion soup, (just enough to moisten the bread), and continue layering until the dish is full. Finish with a layer of cheese. Bake in oven (450°) until well browned.

Serve a portion of casserole in each dish and pass a **terrine** of soup to add to each serving. This soup is far superior to plain onion soup and is a favorite of the central regions of France.

Soupe aux Praires

Clam Soup
6 to 8 servings

1 ½ cups chopped clams,
    fresh or canned
1 medium onion, finely chopped
2 medium potatoes, diced
    in small cubes
1 large tomato, peeled
    and chopped

3 slices fresh salt pork
extra bottled clam juice
    to make 1 quart
3 cups light cream
pinch of thyme
butter
fresh parsley

Steam clams; chop and reserve meat and juice. Boil the strips of fresh salted pork for 10 to 15 minutes, then cut into smaller strips and cook in a skillet over medium heat until quite crisp; remove and drain on paper towels. To the fat in the pan add the finely chopped onion, the diced potatoes and brown lightly. Add chopped tomato and 2 cups of water, and transfer to a pot and cook until tender. Add the pork and clam juice, salt and pepper to taste and simmer 5 minutes; add chopped clams and simmer 5 minutes more. Lastly, add 3 cups of light cream and adjust seasoning. On each serving, put a dollop of fresh butter and a little chopped parsley.

Crab Bisqué

1 large cooked crab
6 tbsps oil and butter for
    sautéeing **mirepoix**
1 quart fish **fumet** or
    fish stock
salt, pepper, cayenne pepper
¹/₃ cup sherry
butter

½ cup each leeks, celery,
    carrots, chopped fine
3 tbsps flour
1 cup white wine
2 small tomatoes, peeled
    and chopped
½ cup cream
fines herbes

Sauté the vegetables slowly in the butter and oil. Add the flour and raise heat, stirring for a few minutes. Then add heated fish *fumet* or fish stock and white wine and stir the soup until it boils. Then simmer the soup slowly for an hour. Add the two tomatoes, peeled and chopped. Take the crab out of its shell, being careful to reserve all the parts for the soup except the lungs and the shell. The brownish liquid next to the shell (the "cream of the crab") is especially flavorful. Stir the crab into the soup with the seasonings and add sherry and cream. Off the heat add butter for enrichment and the herbs. The soup may be thickened with rice if desired; a thicker soup may also be made by using fish **veloute sauce** instead of the fish stock.

Soupe au Pistou   Pasto Soup

Pistou comes from the word "pesto" — a pounding of garlic, basil, and parmesan cheese with the addition of olive oil (of Genoese origin). It is the essential part of the soup.

2 to 3 potatoes
3 to 4 carrots
2 to 3 leeks
one medium onion
3 qts broth (chicken or
   veal), or water
1 cup fresh white beans or
   red beans (dried, precooked
   or canned)
½ lb fresh green
   beans

1 cup fresh green peas
1 cup zucchini, diced
handful broken spaghetti
1 piece stale French bread,
   (optional)
1 large tomato

Pistou: 4 to 5 cloves garlic
   fresh basil
   parmesan cheese
      (¹/₃ to ½ cup)
   ½ cup olive oil
   1 to 2 tomatoes or
      1 tsp tomato paste

Pistou: Pound garlic to a pulp, add basic and pound again; add tomatoes (peeled, seeded, and diced) or tomato paste, and parmesan cheese. Mix all well and work in ½ cup olive oil. This can be made well in advance.

Soup: Sauté leeks, onions, potatoes, and carrots; add the broth, beans (if fresh; if dried must be pre-cooked), and cook for about 10 minutes. About 15 minutes before serving, add string beans, peas, zucchini and tomato (and bread if desired).

Put pistou in a terrine or heavy bowl and add the soup gradually, mixing with the pistou. Add a **chiffonade** of 1 tbsp chopped parsley and basil (tarragon and chervil optional).

Potage St. Hubert   St. Hubert's Soup
                                        (Patron Saint of Hunters)

This soup offers a very good use of game carcasses and bones (wild birds, animals, domestic duck, etc.).

2 to 3 qts broth made from
   carcass and bones of
   birds, animals
1 to 2 carrots diced
2 to 3 leaves of cabbage,
   minced
salt and pepper

2 tbsps barley
½ cup split peas
   (yellow or green)
1 onion (or leek)
   chopped coarsely
¼ cup sherry

Bring barley and peas to a boil, lower heat and simmer for 1 to 1½ hours.

Add the rest of the vegetables and cook for ½ hour more. Serve strained or unstrained with **croutons** of toasted French bread. If some of the meat is left on the bones, dice it up and add to the soup. Add the sherry at the last minute and serve hot.

La Soupe aux Concombres
Cucumber Soup

4 servings

4 small cucumbers
2 tbsps butter
2 tbsps oil
1 to 2 qts **fond blanc**
  (white stock), chicken or
  veal
1 cup bread crumbs
2 small onions, chopped
1 pinch cayenne, salt, pepper,
  nutmeg to taste
1 to 2 cloves garlic, minced

½ cup Bechamel or Velouté
  (See Sauces) or 3 to 4
  tbsps flour
2 egg yolks
½ cup sherry
½ cup heavy cream, or
  sour cream
$^1/_3$ cup grated cheese
Garnish: 1 tbsp chervil,
  tarragon, parsley (combined)

Peel the cucumbers and remove the seeds if too seedy. Plunge them in boiling water for 2 minutes, strain, then cut them into thick slices. Sauté the onion in the butter and oil without allowing it to brown; add the cucumbers and if you do not plan to add Bechamel sauce, add 3 to 4 tbsps flour at this time. Stir in stock, bread crumbs, seasonings and simmer for five minutes. Bechamel can now be added with the sherry and simmer for another five minutes. Strain. Blend egg yolks and cream and add to the soup at the last minute, and top soup with grated cheese, a little butter and fine herbs. Serve very cold.

Soupe aux Exosses de Petits Pois
Pea Pod Soup

2 qts pea pods, washed
  and stemmed
1 small head lettuce, chopped
1 small onion, chopped
6 sprigs parsley
1 tbsp butter

1 tsp salt
3 cups water
1 cup light cream
1 tbsp butter
2 tbsps flour

Combine in a soup kettle the pea pods, lettuce, onion, parsley, one tablespoon butter, salt and water. Bring the mixture to a boil and simmer it for one-half hour. Strain the soup through a fine sieve, forcing the pulp through. Thicken the purée with a mixture of one tablespoon butter and two tablespoons of flour. Bring the soup to a boil, add one cup of light cream and reheat without boiling. Serve hot.

Potage Crème Chàtelaine

Cream of Artichoke Soup
6 to 8 servings

6 artichokes
2 tbsps flour
2 egg yolks
salt and pepper to taste
1 cup heavy cream

2 ozs butter
6 ½ cups of stock
   (beef or chicken)
1 tbsp chervil leaves

Cook artichokes in boiling water (salted) for about 30 to 45 minutes (for large ones). Drain. Take all the leaves off and the choke out. Sauté both in a little butter very lightly but do not brown. In a heavy pan (2½ quarts) melt remaining butter and mix in the flour.

Stir and cook for 1 minute. Add stock and stir until mixture has slightly thickened. Strain sautéed bottoms and flesh from leaves of artichokes (scraping it with a spoon through a fine sieve or putting it into an electric blender with some stock). Add this to the mixture in pan and simmer for 20 minutes more. Taste for seasoning. Beat egg yolks with cream which has been warmed without boiling. Add to soup. Sprinkle with chopped or whole chervil leaves and serve hot. On very warm days, the soup is best eaten cold. This recipe can apply to any other cream (vegetable) soup, e.g., cream of watercress, sorrel, etc.

Potage Choux de Bruxelles à la Flamande
Flemish Brussels Sprouts Soup

1 lb of brussels sprouts
3 to 4 cups of chicken broth
   or other white stock
2 cups milk
2 egg yolks

1 cup of spinach
2 tbsps of butter
¹/₃ cup of flour
2 cups heavy cream
salt, pepper

Cover brussels sprouts with water. Add a little salt and cook for about 10 to 15 minutes. Drain, reserving a few sprouts for garnish. Also cook the spinach in a little salted water for 10 minutes. Purée the two vegetables in a fine seive or in a blender with a little of the stock.

In a sauce pan melt 2 tbsps of butter. Add the flour and slowly add the milk, stirring until smooth. Cook in a double boiler for 15 minutes. Then add to the soup and let it cook another 5 minutes.

Just before serving mix egg yolks with enough cream to dilute. Add to the boiling soup, stir and serve at once.

Garnish with the reserved brussels sprouts and the remaining cream which has been whipped. Or make lemon cups by cutting lemons in half, scooping out the pulp and filling them with whipped cream which has been seasoned with a little salt and put through a rose pastry tube.

Soupe aux Concombres et Betteraves
Cucumber and Beet Soup

1 clove garlic	4 cups sour cream
½ tsp salt	1 cup milk
2 cups cucumber, finely chopped	2 tsps each chopped parsley and chives
1 cup cooked beets, chopped	salt and pepper
	a few cucumber slices

Chop finely one clove of garlic and mix thoroughly with finely chopped cucumber, one-half tsp salt, and chopped cooked beets. Mix in sour cream, milk, parsley and chives, and salt and pepper to taste. Chill the soup and serve it with a few thin cucumber slices and an ice cube in each soup plate.

Bouillabaisse de Marseille   Fish Soup Provençale

Marseille is the mother of Bouillabaisse. Fish available there are not found even in other parts of France, so select the fish of your area for this soup. Because of the variety of fish required, even in small quantity, Bouillabaisse should be made for no less than 6 people.

6 to 8 lbs shellfish (crab, lobster, prawns, clams, as you wish)	2 cups white wine
	2 cups fish *fumet* (court bouillon of fish, heads, bones)
2 leeks	⅛ tsp saffon, salt, pepper
1 large onion	dash of cayenne, thyme
2 or 3 tomatoes	3 or 4 cloves garlic, crushed
bay leaf	parsley, chopped
½ cup olive oil	1 to 2 pieces orange or lemon peel
butter	
slices of fried French bread (1 per serving)	

Wash and slice leeks and onion. Sauté in olive oil and butter without browning. Slice all the fish and stir them into onion and leeks. Add tomatoes, wine, stock, bay leaf, seasonings, orange peel. Cook on high fire for 20 to 25 minutes. Take fish out and keep warm.

Fry slices of bread in olive oil and butter until golden brown. Put one slice of bread on each plate; cover with fish and pour soup over, or serve soup over the bread and the fish on the side. Sprinkle with parsley.

Potage Vichyssoise Josephine

Potato Soup Josephine
6 servings

4 medium potatoes
4 leeks, white part only
1 large onion, chopped
2 tbsps butter or bacon fat
1 tbsp flour
2 qts chicken or veal broth

¼ cup butter or margarine
¹/₃ cup pastry cream (half and half)
 or canned milk for leeks
²/₃ cup cream, to add when done
salt, pepper, nutmeg
1 tbsp chives, chopped

Peel and rinse the potatoes and boil them with one quart of broth for 25 to 30 minutes.

Meanwhile wash the leeks thoroughly and chop them. Sauté the leeks and the onion in butter or bacon fat, without allowing them to brown. Add 1 tbsp flour, then add some of the warm broth gradually to prevent lumps. Add about 2 cups of broth. Cook, covered, for about 25 to 30 minutes on a low heat. When done, purée in a blender.

When the potatoes are cooked, strain them, saving the cooking broth. Mash the potatoes and add ¼ cup butter or margarine and ¹/₃ cup of cream. Mix in the puréed onion and leek mixture. Now add all the remaining broth, let it come to a boil, and add the remaining cream. Remove from the heat.

Serve very hot or very cold, sprinkled with chives.

Potage aux Herbes

Herb Soup
6 servings

¼ lb sorrel
small bunch of watercress
 leaves and stems (optional)
1 small onion
¼ lb spinach (1 cup)
1 medium potato, diced
3 tbsps butter or margarine
1½ qts chicken or veal stock
salt, pepper
2 egg yolks
chiffonade of lettuce,
 watercress or both

1 tbsp each of tarragon,
 parsley, chives, chervil,
 sweet basil
sprig each of fresh thyme,
 marjoram or oregano
 (or 1 tbsp each)
1 tbsp flour
1 tbsp *razed* of minute Tapioca
⅛ tbsp nutmeg
½ cup cream or condensed
 milk

Chop onion and sauté in butter or margarine until translucent but not brown; add flour and stir. Add sorrel, spinach, potato, herbs, stock, salt, pepper, nutmeg, and simmer for 25 to 30 minutes. Strain through a fine sieve or blender. Return to pot and bring to a boil; then add the tapioca dissolved in a little stock, and cook for 2 to 3 minutes more until the tapioca is translucent. Taste for seasoning. Shred lettuce or watercress for the chiffonade and add to the soup. Cook 2 to 3 minutes longer and remove from heat. Make a **liaison** with beaten egg yolks and the cream, stirred into the soup. Serve hot or cold.

Potage aux Courgettes

Squash Soup
6 to 8 servings

¼ cup butter (½ cube)
1 large onion, chopped
2 lbs zucchini or other squash
3 rounded tbsps farina
  (couscous kind)
2 qts chicken broth,
  heated

1 cup sorrel, chopped
1 tsp fennel green and
  tarragon, chopped
salt and pepper to taste
pinch of nutmeg
½ cup cream
1 egg yolk

Melt the butter and sauté the chopped onion without letting it brown. Add the zucchini and farina and stir. Add the hot broth and cook for 20 to 25 minutes, then add the sorrel and herbs and cook 5 minutes more.

Put the mixture through a sieve or in a blender. Return it to the pot and bring it to a boil. Add salt, pepper and nutmeg to taste.

Mix the egg yolk with the cream and add it to the soup at the last minute before serving. Do not allow the soup to boil after adding the egg yolk and cream.

VEGETABLES

966. - PONT-SCORFF

La Vallée du Scorff

Collection H. Laurent, Port-Louis

Grandmere's House

Vegetables

I owe my good health ~ as well as my love of cooking ~ to my grandmother. There was nothing artificial about her or the food she prepared. Since I was seven years old, until I was twenty, I worked in her garden and watched her cook. She had a lot of land next to the river in Pont Scorff, near Lorient, in Brittany. She was land rich, with a huge garden full of fruits and vegetables. There was no bath tub ~ we used to bathe in the river every day.

Grandmère taught me how to cook. My mother didn't have time for gardening and cooking, what with raising eight children and being a professional tailor. My grandmother would frequently mix vegetables with fruit, and we used to tell her, "Grandma, that's kind of goofy!" But today such combinations do not seem so strange. She made rutabaga with quinces, fresh cherries with string beans, kumquat with Jerusalem artichokes, red cabbage with blueberries, rhubarb with swiss chard, turnips with figs. She had an incredible talent and imagination in combining different flavors. She never used wine in her cookery, but she cooked an awful lot with cider. She cooked her hams ~ even the fresh eels from the river ~ in cider. I used to watch everything she did ~ she couldn't read or write, but she was as sharp as a butcher knife. This I learned from her: my formal training was to come much later when I went to Paris.

Topinambours aux Herbes

Jerusalem Artichokes with Herbs

1 large potato, cooked and mashed
1 lb Jerusalem artichokes
¼ cup butter

2 tbsps herbs: mixture of parsley, chives, tarragon, chervil, basil
salt, pepper, nutmeg

Boil and mash the potato.
Boil the Jerusalem artichokes for 5 to 6 minutes. Peel them and boil again

Continued

for 10 minutes. Mash and add the butter, herbs, and mashed potato. Season with salt, pepper, and nutmeg. Serve hot, and is especially good with chicken, lamb, and veal.

Haricots de la Côte Atlantique   Dry Beans Atlantic
4 to 6 servings

1 lb dry beans (navy or
   Great Western)
¼ lb smoked or fresh bacon
   (in one piece)
2 tbsps butter
2 tbsps oil

1 lb fresh tomatoes, chopped
salt and pepper
⅛ tsp rosemary
1 sprig thyme
parsley, chopped
1 onion, sliced

Wash the beans before soaking. Soak overnight; reserve the soaking liquid.

Cook the beans in their liquid, without salt. Bring them to a boil, reduce the heat and cook for 45 minutes. Add the bacon and cook 15 minutes more. Take out the bacon and dice it. Sauté the diced bacon in butter and oil. Add the sliced onion and chopped tomatoes. When all is browned, add it to the beans and simmer a few minutes. Add salt and pepper, chopped rosemary and thyme. The beans should have absorbed the liquid but should not have burst.

Serve sprinkled with parsley.

HINT: COOKING DRIED VEGETABLES

When cooking dried beans (and other vegetables), do not put salt into the cooking water or the beans will burst, and will not be as presentable as they would be whole. *The exception to the rule* is when making bean soup or purée — add salt to the water to facilitate the puréeing process.

Fleur de Broccoli Vinaigrette   Broccoli Vinaigrette

broccoli flowerettes, washed
3 tbsps oil
1 tbsp vinegar
1 tsp prepared mustard

pepper to taste (large pinch)
salt to taste
1 tbsp chives
1 tbsp parsley

Cook flowerettes in boiling water, adding salt when the water comes back to a boil, for 10 to 15 minutes.

Prepare a vinaigrette sauce with the remaining ingredients and pour the sauce over the hot, drained vegetables.

HINT: Cabbage

To take away the strong taste of cabbage, add to the cooking water a piece of bread (rye especially) to absorb the bitterness and odor of the cabbage. Do not cook the core of the cabbage.

To avoid the strong odor of cabbage while it is cooking, cover the lid with a towel soaked in vinegar.

Green cabbage and cauliflower should be fresh and very firm and without blemishes when picked; brussel sprouts should be picked at the end of the season, or when their leaves are yellow.

Chou Blanc au Gratin / White Cabbage Casserole

1 ½ to 2 lbs cabbage
4 medium onions
2 cloves garlic
¼ cup butter
½ lb ground meat (beef, veal, pork, chicken — any meat on hand)
4 tomatoes, peeled and chopped
2 tbsps tomato paste
2 sprigs fresh thyme
bay leaf
salt and pepper
2 tbsps bacon drippings
breadcrumbs

Trim, wash and mince cabbage; blanch in boiling water for 7 to 8 minutes. Drain and set aside. Peel and chop the onions and garlic and sauté in butter until lightly browned. Add the meat, tomatoes, tomato paste, and seasonings. Cook on low heat for about 20 minutes. Sauté the cabbage in the bacon drippings.

In an oven proof dish, layer alternately the cabbage and meat mixture. Sprinkle with breadcrumbs, dot with butter and warm in the oven for 10 minutes. Then place under broiler to brown.

Chou Rouge à la Flamande / Red Cabbage Flanders Style

1 to 2 lbs red cabbage
4 tbsps bacon fat
2 large onions, coarsely chopped
2 peeled and diced apples
½ cup red wine vinegar
2 level tbsps brown sugar
½ tsp nutmeg
thyme, bay leaf
salt and pepper

Wash and cut cabbage into quarters. Melt bacon fat and add cabbage, onions, and cook until vegetables are translucent but not brown. Add the apples and moisten with vinegar, brown sugar and seasonings. If necessary, add broth or water to cover and cook very slowly for 1 hour.

HINT:

Never put salt in the water before putting in the vegetables. When the water boils with the salt, there is a reaction which is not good for the vegetables. However, vegetables may be sprinkled with salt before they are plunged into the boiling water.

Artichauts à la Bretonne

Artichokes, Brittany Style
4-6 servings

8 artichokes
3 cloves garlic, chopped
1 tbsp parsley, chopped
1 tbsp mint, chopped

salt and pepper
4 tbsps oil
1 cup wine
½ cup bouillon

Remove the tough outer leaves from the artichokes and cut off ½ inch from the top of the leaves to remove all the prickly points.

Mix the garlic and herbs, salt and pepper, and place this stuffing between the leaves.

Place the artichokes side by side in a fireproof dish, pour the oil over them and cook, covered, for 10 minutes over very low heat. Pour the wine and bouillon over, and continue cooking, covered, for 45 minutes longer. By this time the liquid should be almost completely reduced and the artichokes tender.

Asperges en Petit Pois

Chopped Asparagus

1 bunch asparagus stalks
¼ cup butter or margarine
salt and pepper
a soupçon (pinch) cayenne pepper

the green of 1 scallion (optional)
2 tbsps heavy cream or
   condensed milk
juice of half lemon

Cut the stalks (already peeled and washed) into pea-size pieces. Melt butter or margerine in heavy pot and add the asparagus, salt, pepper, cayenne. Cook, then lower heat and add scallion, and cook for about 7 minutes. Add the cream, gently shaking pot to mix for a minute, and serve, squeezing lemon juice over it at the last minute.

 HINT:

The asparagus should never be cut with a knife — break the stalk at the tenderest spot, using your thumb and index fingers. After breaking and drying the stalks, they may be cut with a knife as desired.

American cooks, as a rule, do not peel asparagus; the French always do — they also cook them much faster, thus making the entire stalk edible. When cooking the entire stalks, tie them in bunches and stand them on end in the pot.

Haricots Verts Bordelaises

Green Beans with Wine and Grapes

1 ½ to 2 lbs green beans
½ cup red wine vinegar or red wine
   with 2 tbsps vinegar to total
   ½ cup, reduce the ½ cup
   to about 2 tbsps over high heat

2 egg yolks
salt, pepper, butter, parsley
   for garnish
Muscats, if possible
3 tbsps heavy cream

Slice beans lengthwise. Cook in boiling water. Toss cooked beans with 1 to 2 tbsps slightly browned butter and grapes.

Just before serving, mix egg yolks and cream, add salt and pepper. Stir into hot reduced wine. Pour over beans. Serve.

Haricots Verts Montmorency

Green Beans with Cherries

1 lb green beans
½ lb cherries

6 tbsps butter
salt and pepper

Cook green beans in boiling water about 10 to 15 minutes, or until tender.

Pit the cherries. Melt butter. Toss cherries in butter until well coated and warmed. Add to cooked beans. Toss. Salt and pepper to taste.

Carottes et Apricots
Carrots with Apricots

1 lb carrots
½ lb apricots, halved
butter
1 tsp sugar

1 dozen green olives
salt and pepper
parsley

Slice the carrots and cook in boiling water for 10 to 15 minutes (remember: no salt added to the water until after water has begun to boil). Strain and add butter and sugar.

Add green olives that have been tossed in butter. Also add the apricots (peeled or unpeeled) after they have been sautéed in butter. Serve with salt, pepper and parsley.

Chou-Fleur en Fritots
Cauliflower Fritters

Bechamel sauce (see Sauces)
⅓ cup grated cheese
1 large cauliflower
1 tbsp flour
2 tbsps white vinegar or lemon juice

1 tsp salt
flour, for coating the fritters
1 egg, beaten
bread crumbs for coating fritters
oil for deep frying

Make a Bechamel sauce and add ⅓ cup grated cheese.

Meanwhile, fill a large pot with water, add the flour diluted with a little water, and the vinegar or lemon juice. Bring it to a boil, then add the cauliflower and salt. Cook about 15 minutes, until just tender (the cauliflower should still be slightly crisp — do not overcook). Drain and chop the cauliflower and add to the Bechamel. Let it cool.

When cool, cut the mixture into pieces and shape each like a small sausage. Roll in flour, then dip into the beaten egg, and then in the bread crumbs. Fry in the hot fat until browned. Drain on absorbent paper, set on a warm platter and serve garnished with a bouquet of parsley in the center. Serve a light tomato sauce separately.

Note: This dish can be made with *leftover* cauliflower.

Courgettes au Vert
Zucchini with Greens
6 to 8 servings

3 lbs zucchini
2 heads of green lettuce (Boston)
2 bunches of sorrel or spinach

2 chopped shallots very fine
¼ cup butter
2 tbsps oil or margarine

Shred the zucchini on the coarsest hole of the grater, (they should be a little thicker than a match) put in bowl with 1 tsp of salt and let it stand 15 to 20 minutes, to eliminate their water content. *Drain.* Put in colander over running water to take out all possible salt. Dry well. Meanwhile trim and wash the greens chosen. Dry and chop not too fine or too coarse; melt ½ of the butter and oil in a pan, toss the greens in it and simmer a few minutes until tender; add salt, pepper, nutmeg to taste.

Take greens out of pan and reserve. In the same pan, add remaining butter and oil, when hot add shallots and zucchini, toss and stir, cook over low heat for about 10 minutes; add the greens and warm through. Serve in vegetable dish, with any kind of roast, fowl, boiled or broiled fish and steamed potatoes.

Celeri Rave Sauce Normande

Celery Root with Normandy Sauce
4 to 6 servings

2 large or 3 or 4 small
  celery roots
lemon juice

butter
Sauce Normande
1 tbsp chervil or parsley

Boil the celery root for 15 to 20 minutes or until tender but crisp. Peel. Marinate it in lemon juice until ready to use. Prepare the **Sauce Normande** (see *Sauces*).

Before serving, dice the celery root and heat it in melted butter. Put it in a warm serving dish, cover with **Sauce Normande,** and garnish with herbs.

Note: Cooked celery root is also nice in salads. Cook and marinate as above. Make a vinaigrette sauce and add to it the sieved yolk of a hard-boiled egg, capers, mustard, and the lemon juice from the marinade.

Aubergines Grillées

Grilled Eggplant
4 to 6 servings

2 eggplants
oil
2 cloves of garlic, minced

brown butter
parsley, chopped
salt and pepper

Wash and dry the eggplants and cut them into even slices. Rub the slices with oil and broil them in a preheated broiler for 7 to 10 minutes on each side. Sprinkle with minced garlic, browned butter, parsley, and salt and pepper before serving.

Tartines d'Aubergines

Eggplant Sandwich
4 to 6 servings

2 eggplants
salt and pepper
¼ lb Gruyere cheese, sliced
12 anchovy fillets
flour

1 egg, beaten
bread crumbs
oil for frying
1 lemon, cut into wedges
parsley, chopped

Continued

Wash the eggplants and cut them lengthwise into even slices. Season each slice with salt and pepper and top one half of the slices with a slice of cheese and a few anchovy fillets. Top with the remaining slices to make sandwiches.

Roll the eggplant sandwiches in flour, then dip them in beaten egg and finally in bread crumbs. Fry in hot oil until browned on both sides. Serve with a piece of anchovy on top of each, garnished with lemon wedges and chopped parsley.

Chausson aux Champignons

Mushroom Turnovers

6 to 8 servings

1 lb mushrooms, finely sliced
3 tbsps butter
1 tbsp oil
salt and pepper
1 tbsp parsley, chopped

1 clove garlic, finely chopped
$^1/_3$ cup heavy cream
1 egg yolk, mixed with
  a little cream
1 recipe of Pâte brisée fine.

Heat the butter and oil and sauté the finely sliced mushrooms until soft, about 5 minutes. Season with salt and pepper, add the chopped parsley and garlic and cook for 1 to 2 minutes. Add the cream and the egg yolk which has been mixed with a little cream. Let the mixture cool. When cool, preheat oven to 375⁰.

Make a recipe of pâte brisée, rolling the dough $^1/_8''$ thick. Cut into small rounds. Place a rounded spoonful of the cooled filling on the top half of each round and fold the bottom half over it to make semicircular turnovers. Press the edges together firmly.

Bake the turnovers in a 375⁰ oven for about 30 minutes.

Oignons Farcis

Stuffed Onions

12 large onions
$^1/_3$ cup raw rice
1 veal kidney (or lamb) well
  cleaned. If necessary use ½
  beef kidney which has been parboiled for a milder flavor
$^1/_3$ cup parmesan cheese
1 cup sour or heavy cream
½ lb apricots, peeled, pitted, crushed
½ lb cup bread crumbs

¼ cup sherry
½ cup chopped parsley
2 tbsps basil (or pesto)
1 tbsp tarragon
pinches oregano, sage, marjaram
3 to 4 tbsps melted butter
¼ to ½ cup bouillon
salt and pepper
tomato sauce

Core onions with grapefruit knife. Reserve cores — you will need some for this dish — use the rest for onion soup or whatever. Place onions, cavity up, in large pan of boiling water to cover. Add salt, cook covered 7 minutes. Use onion water to cook rice. (Onions will fit nicely, 6 at a time in 5 qt pot.) Sauté enough onion pulp, chopped, to yield 1 cup.

Sauté in melted butter the kidney, finely chopped, the cooked rice and sautéd onion pulp. Add 1 tsp salt and ½ tsp pepper. Transfer to bowl and add bread crumbs, cheese, herbs, cream, sherry and apricots. Stuffing should be moist.

Brush cavities of parboiled onions with melted butter. Lightly salt and pepper each one. Fill with stuffing mixture. Sprinkle tops with more bread crumbs and cheese. Place a small piece of butter on each. Put onions in buttered baking pan. Add bouillon to bottom of pan. Bake 375° for 1 to 1½ hours. Cover with foil if they brown before they are tender. Serve with a little tomato sauce on each one.

Pommes de Terre au Rocquefort

Potato with Roquefort Cheese

1½ lbs potatoes
¼ lb Roquefort cheese
1 cup milk
salt and pepper

¼ cup butter
1 egg yolk
⅓ cup heavy cream

Preheat oven to 325°.

Peel and wash the potatoes. Mash the Roquefort with a fork and mix, little by little, with the milk until it becomes liquid. Season with a very little salt and more pepper.

Grease an ovenproof dish. Slice the potatoes very thin and arrange a layer of potatoes in the bottom of the dish, then a layer of Roquefort cream, then more potatoes, more Roquefort cream until all is used. Finish with potatoes on top. Dot with butter, cover and bake at 325° for 1 hour.

Mix the egg yolk with the cream and a little pepper. Pour this mixture over the potatoes and let them cook for ½ hour more, uncovered at 300°. At the end of this time the dish should be just browned and the potatoes very tender.

Pommes de Terre à l'Aigée

Sour Mashed Potatoes

1 to 2 lbs potatoes, boiled and peeled
1 cup sour cream
2 tbsps goose or other fat
oil and vinegar (3 to 1 tbsp)
salt and pepper

1 tsp prepared mustard
Worcestershire sauce
pinch **aromatic herbs**
tarragon
chives

Save water from boiled potatoes for soup.

Add butter to potatoes and purée. Add oil, vinegar, few drops of Worcestershire, mustard, salt and pepper, 1 good pinch of **aromatic herbs,** 1 tsp each of tarragon and chives. Add sour cream, mix and serve.

Pommes de Terre Macaire
(Auguste Escoffier)

Sautéed Baked Potatoes

baking potatoes (large)
½ stick of butter

salt, pepper, nutmeg
clarified butter for frying

Bake potatoes in a 450° oven for three-quarters to one hour. Cut in two and scoop out the pulp. Mash this pulp while mixing in two ounces of butter. Season with salt, pepper, and nutmeg. Put potato pulp into a frying pan and sauté in clarified butter, spreading the potato out like a pancake. Fry until golden brown on both sides. Serve on a round dish and cut into portions. These potatoes may also be made in small cakes for individual servings.

Pommes de Terre Dauphine

Dauphine Potatoes
4 to 6 servings

1 lb of Dutchess potatoes
  (see *Culinary Glossary*)
½ recipe of pâte à choux
  (see *Pastry Dough*)

⅛ tsp pepper
⅛ tsp nutmeg (or to taste)
fat for deep drying
½ tsp salt

Make a recipe of Duchess potatoes and one-half recipe of pâte à choux. Mix them together, adding salt, pepper and nutmeg to taste. Let the mixture cool enough to be formed into small balls (or use a spoon). Drop into deep hot fat and cook until brown.

Drain on absorbent paper and serve around dish, in a vegetable dish, or heaped on a napkin.

Note: These potato balls can be made in different shapes. They can be dipped in egg and breadcrumbs, if desired. Butter and oil may be used instead of the deep fat.

Rutabaga with Quinces
4 servings

1 lb of rutabaga
½ lb of quinces (peeled)
⅓ cup of white wine

salt and pepper
butter

Cook rutabaga in boiling water 30 to 45 minutes until tender. Cook the quinces separately in the wine, 2 tbsp butter, salt and pepper for ten minutes. Drain the rutabaga and add 2 tbsp butter. Mix in quinces, sprinkle with parsley, and serve.

Timbales d'Épinards

Spinach Timbales

2 lbs fresh spinach or 2 packages
  (10 oz each) of frozen
3 tbsps flour
2 oz butter
½ pint heavy cream
½ cup milk
1 egg yolk
1 whole egg

2 egg whites
salt, pepper and nutmeg to taste
½ tsp dried thyme or ½ tsp
  chopped fresh thyme
Sauce Velouté (optional) (see *Sauces*)
1 cup bread crumbs
1 small onion chopped
small baba molds or pyrex
  custard cups

If frozen spinach is used, cook it according to package directions. If fresh spinach is used, wash it thoroughly. Drain and place it in a saucepan with very little water. Cover and cook over moderately low heat until spinach is tender. Drain and press out water. Chop spinach fine, or put it through a blender, add bread crumbs and set aside.

Melt butter in a 1-quart saucepan, add chopped onion, stir until soft; add flour, stir for 1 minute and then add warm milk and cream. Stir until the sauce is thick. Add spinach and bread crumbs. Add egg yolk and whole egg beaten, salt, pepper, nutmeg and thyme. Mix well. Beat egg whites until they stand in soft peaks and fold them into the mixture. Turn into individual molds. Bake in a preheated oven (350º) for ½ hour in a pan of water. Test the timbales by inserting a small knife in the center. If the knife comes out clean, they are done. Let them stand in the molds for five minutes, then unmold on the serving dish as a garnish.

Serve with Sauce Velouté if desired.

Pain d'Épinards aux Foies de Poulet

Spinach Loaf with Chicken Livers
4 to 6 servings

This dish may be served for dinner as a first course or for luncheon with a green salad.

1 lb spinach, washed
2 tbsps sherry
1 medium onion, chopped
4 tbsps butter
2 rounded tbsps flour
¾ cup milk, approximately

salt, pepper and nutmeg to taste
2 eggs, separated
½ cup bread crumbs
pinch of thyme
1 lb chicken livers
¹/₃ cup sherry for deglazing
1½ cups Sauce Velouté (see *Sauces*)

Preheat oven to 350º.

Cook spinach very slowly in 2 tbsps sherry. Drain, reserving juices (if any), and chop very fine. Set spinach aside.

Continued

Make a sauce by sautéing onion in butter until transparent, not brown. Add flour and cook for 1 minute, stirring. Then add reserved spinach liquid along with just enough milk (¾ cup) to make a thick sauce. Season with salt, pepper and nutmeg.

Combine spinach, egg yolks, bread crumbs and thyme with the sauce.

Sauté chicken livers and set aside ¾ of them. Cut each of the remaining livers into four slices and add to spinach mixture.

Beat egg whites until stiff. Fold ⅓ portion into spinach mixture, combining well, and then fold in the rest, gently.

Pour into greased mold (ring, round, oval or charlotte) and bake in a preheated oven for about 45 minutes.

Unmold spinach on warm platter and surround with chicken livers. (For a ring mold put livers or carrots or mushrooms in center.) On the side serve Sauce Velouté, adding to it the chicken liver juices deglazed with sherry and reduced.

Blettes à la Voironnaise

Swiss Chard with Egg and Cheese
4 to 6 servings

2 bunches Swiss chard
1 medium onion, chopped
¼ cup butter
1 egg

⅓ cup cream
salt, pepper and nutmeg
¼ cup Swiss cheese, grated
2 to 3 tbsps Bechamel Sauce
   (see *Sauces*)

Wash the Swiss chard and boil for 10 minutes, then drain and chop. Sauté chopped onion in butter, add the Swiss chard and mix well. Beat the egg with the cream and add to the chard, along with salt, pepper and nutmeg to taste. Add the grated cheese and bind with Bechamel Sauce. Serve hot.

Turnips with Figs
4 servings

1 lb white turnips
½ lb figs
salt and pepper

butter
parsley

Cook the turnips in water for ten minutes; drain. Coat in 2 tbsps butter, and salt and pepper. Smear the raw figs with 2 tbsps butter and add to the turnips. Serve with parsley.

Courgettes de Paul

Paul's Zucchini
4 servings

6 zucchini, medium size
Fine herbs: basil, parsley, tarragon,
   chervil and green of fennel
3 to 4 tbsps butter, melted

3 tbsps oil
1 tbsp vinegar
1 tsp strong mustard
salt, pepper

Do not peel the zucchini; cut them in half lengthwise and remove the seeds and some of the flesh. Reserve the flesh. Blanch the zucchini shells for 5 minutes in boiling water; take out and drain.

Chop the reserved zucchini flesh and all the herbs. Sauté in butter. Make a vinaigrette with the oil, vinegar, mustard, salt and pepper and season with zucchini mixture. Fill the zucchini shells and serve cold.

CHEESE AND EGG DISHES

CREATURE ATTACHMENTS

Cheese and Egg Dishes

I worked for several of San Francisco's wealthiest and most prominent families, some of whom were far from extravagant in managing their households. I remember one very grand lady who ordered a pound of Roquefort cheese for a dinner party she was giving. Her husband's family happened to control the imports of food into the West Coast from Europe. After the meal, there was one small piece of that cheese left, which I wrapped and put in the refrigerator ~ I wasn't going to throw it away, of course!

About eight o'clock the next morning the chauffeur came into the kitchen. It was raining and very cold outside, so he asked for a drink. I told him that if the mistress smelled liquor on his breath, she would fire him immediately. But then I remembered that little bit of left-over cheese, and gave it to him to buffer the alcohol. He ate the cheese, had the drink he wanted, and went off to his chauffeuring. I didn't think anything more about the incident.

Noon came and the lady announced she would like the Roquefort with her lunch. Rather than make trouble for the chauffeur, I told the maid to say to her that I had eaten the cheese. After lunch the woman came into the kitchen to see me. "Josephine, I want you to under-stand, I do not buy imported cheese for my help." Imploring the assistance of the Holy Spirit, I was suddenly inspired to answer her back, "But Madam, I am imported too." I thought she would fire me, but that was the last I ever heard of it, and I stayed with her two more years. Shortly after this incident, I received a rather large raise!

Song to Beat Eggs and Sauces to:

Et pendant ce temps là
Je tournais la Manivelle
et monsieur jouait de la prunelle
comme un gros pacha

M. Pellaprat's song

Soufflé aux Herbes du Jardin

Cheese Soufflé with Herbs

4 tbsps butter or margarine
4 dessert spoons of flour (level)
1 cup milk
salt and pepper to taste
⅛ tsp nutmeg
½ cup grated cheese of any
  non-processed kind: Cheddar,
  Monterey, Jack, Swiss, etc.
4 eggs separated,
  2 extra whites

½ tbsp each parsley and chervil
1 sprig each thyme and marjoram,
  or oregano, 1 large sage leaf,
  1 sprig summer savory or
  winter savory
⅛ tbsp fennel leaves
3-qt soufflé mold or
  pyrex greased and coated with
  grated cheese, parmesan,
  or others.

Melt the butter in a double boiler, add flour and stir, cooking for 2 to 3 minutes. Gradually add warm milk with salt, pepper and nutmeg. Cover and cook over simmering water for 15 to 20 minutes. Remove from heat and add the yolks, one at a time, stirring after each is added. Add all of the herbs chopped very fine, the cheese, and fold in egg whites (beaten stiff but not dry).

Fill mold ¾ full, set in middle rack of the oven on a cookie sheet and bake at 375° for 20 to 25 minutes. The center should be very moist when done. Serve "as is," without a sauce.

Soufflé au Fromage et Champignons

Cheese Soufflé with Mushrooms

½ cube butter
⅓ cup flour
1 cup milk, warmed
½ cup grated cheese
  (Swiss, Gruyere, Cheddar, etc.)
6 egg whites
4 egg yolks
½ lb mushrooms, chopped —
  not too fine

2 to 3 large garlic cloves, minced
2 to 3 tbsps chopped fresh herbs:
  parsley, fennel, tarragon,
  chives, etc.
¼ cup butter and 1 tbsp olive oil
  to sauté mushrooms
salt, pepper, nutmeg
butter and Parmesan cheese

Melt butter in top of double boiler, over medium heat. Stir in flour and add warmed milk, little at a time. Mix well. Season with salt, pepper, and nutmeg to taste. Cover and cook over low fire for 20 to 25 minutes. Meanwhile, butter a 1½ qt soufflé or suitable mold and sprinkle with Parmesan cheese. Set aside.

Sauté mushrooms in butter and oil combination. Add garlic, herbs, and season with salt and pepper. Beat egg whites until stiff. Remove the sauce from the fire and beat in the yolks, one at a time. Stir in the cheese. Add one third of the beaten whites and fold to lighten the mixture. Gently fold in half of the remaining whites. Fold in the rest of whites. Pour half of this mixture into the soufflé mold. Gently place the mushrooms over. Add the rest of soufflé mixture. Place on the middle rack of a preheated 375° oven and bake for 20 to 25 minutes.

Quiche Lorraine

Bacon Tart with Cream and Eggs

6 to 8 servings

Originally the Quiche Lorraine was made with fresh lean bacon cut in strips and sautéed very slowly. Many people have adopted ham instead. There are no rules. Use whichever meat you prefer; the procedure is the same.

6 to 8 oz bacon, ham or
    fresh lean bacon
4 eggs
1 ½ cups heavy cream; or
    half milk, half cream
a little salt

⅛ tsp white pepper
⅛ tsp nutmeg
4 tbsps butter
Pâte Brisée for a 9 inch
    pie plate or flan ring
$^1/_3$ to ½ cup grated swiss cheese
    (optional)

If bacon is to be used, blanch in simmering water for 10 minutes to remove salt. If fresh bacon is used, it should be simmered in water for at least an hour, dried, cooled and cut in thin strips.

In the meantime, line a pie or quiche dish with Pâte Brisée reaching ½" above the rim. Be sure to press dough flat against bottom and sides of the pie plate so as to leave no space for air. Lightly prick the bottom and sides of crust with a fork. Line the crust with buttered foil and weigh it down with dried beans. Bake crust in a preheated 375⁰ oven for 10 minutes. Then remove foil and beans and bake for 10 minutes more until the bottom of the crust is light brown.

Warm the cream in a double boiler until almost to the boiling point. (This cuts the cooking time of the quiche by 8 to 10 minutes.) In half the butter, sauté bacon, ham or fresh bacon without browning, just enough to coat in butter. Beat eggs with seasonings and mix with the hot cream. Put bacon and grated cheese in bottom of cooked crust and pour egg mixture over it. Dot quiche with the remaining butter. Do not fill the crust to the very top.

Place quiche on a baking sheet in the upper third of a preheated 375⁰ oven. Bake for 20 to 25 minutes or until a knife inserted in the center comes out clean. Cut in wedges and serve hot as an appetizer, first course, or luncheon dish.

 HINT:

Never throw cheese away. Let it dry out and then grate it.

Tarte au Fromage Herbes

Herbed Cheese Tart
6 servings

Pâte Brisée for a 9″ pie
  pan, baked for 15 minutes
  at 375⁰
1 ½ cups cheese (combine cottage
  cheese and cream cheese,
  whirled smooth in the blender)

½ tsp nutmeg
salt and pepper to taste
2 tbsps (heaping) **fines herbs,**
  chopped
½ tsp **aromatic herbs,** chopped
3 or 4 whole eggs, beaten
2 egg whites, beaten with a
  pinch of salt

Prepare the prebaked Pâte Brisée. Reduce oven heat to 350⁰.

Mix all the ingredients for the filling except the beaten egg whites. After thoroughly mixing other ingredients, fold in the whites. Pour the filling into the pie crust.

Bake for 30 to 35 minutes at 350⁰.

Fondue Savoyarde

Cheese Fondue

1 clove garlic
3 lbs coarsely grated cheese*
⅓ cup kirsch or cognac

2 cups dry white wine
pepper, nutmeg
1 tsp potato or corn starch (rounded)

*The fondue is better if made with two kinds of cheese, one richer in fat than the other — such as gruyère and emmenthaler.

Chop garlic very fine or rub pot in which the cheese is to be fondued. Put pot over hot water. Add two cups of dry white wine. When hot add the cheese, stir it constantly until it melts and becomes creamy. Season to taste with pepper and nutmeg (very little salt, the cheese is already salty). Dilute potato or corn starch in a little wine and add to the cheese stirring. Add the kirsch, and keep the fondue hot in a chafing dish. Dip in pieces of bread or toast with a fork turning well to coat.

 ## HINT: Poached Eggs

Poach eggs in enough water to cover, adding 1 tbsp white vinegar for each quart, to keep eggs from discoloring and to help them coagulate. Do not salt the water as it will uncoagulate the eggs.

Poached eggs can be kept for 2 to 3 days in the refrigerator in cold water. If they are to be served cold, simply drain on a towel; to be served hot, dip them for a minute in very hot water.

Oeufs Poches Florentine

Poached Eggs Florentine
6 servings

2 bunches fresh spinach, cooked
6 eggs for poaching
1 tbsp vinegar for each qt water
4 tbsps of butter
$1/_3$ cup of flour
bread slices (1 per poached egg)

1 cup milk, heated
4 eggs, separated
$1/_8$ tsp each salt,
   pepper and nutmeg
$1/_2$ cup grated cheese (Swiss or
   other whole cheese)

Preheat oven to 375⁰.

Soufflé mixture: Melt 4 tbsps of butter in double boiler, add flour and mix well. Add warm milk slowly and stir until a satiny paste forms. It should be very thick. Remove from heat. Add yolks, one at a time, and season with salt, pepper, nutmeg. Beat egg whites until stiff and fold into yolk mixture gently. Add grated cheese.

Wash and boil spinach, 7 to 10 minutes, adding salt to the boiling water. Drain and chop coarsely, and season with butter, nutmeg, salt and pepper. Moisten with 1 to 2 tbsps of the soufflé mixture and keep warm.

In a skillet, poach the eggs in hot water and vinegar for 2½ to 3 minutes. Take out carefully with slotted spoon and set in cold water to stop the cooking. Set on a towel to dry.

Cut bread slices to the size of the poached eggs and fry in butter. Then place each slice in buttered fire-proof dish, cover first with spinach, then with an egg. Top with cheese mixture. Bake in preheated oven for 15 minutes. When soufflé is done the eggs will be hot but not overcooked.

Oeuf Marçel Argenteuil

Poached Eggs with Asparagus

2 small bunches asparagus
1 egg per serving
2 cups **Bechamel Sauce** (see *Sauces*)

tarragon or watercress leaves
salt and pepper

Wash and peel the asparagus. Break the stalks by hand, then cut into pea-size pieces. Sauté in butter (or 2 tbsps of chicken broth) until tender, about 7 to 10 minutes; salt and pepper and set aside.

Place eggs in boiling water for 5 minutes — no longer. Make a slight crack (to prevent the yolk from darkening) in each egg with a fork or knife or rap eggs on the edge of the counter, and set in cold water. Allow to cool and peel them carefully, as egg will be soft inside. Keep in warm water. Make a Bechamel sauce.

To assemble, put asparagus in bottom of a ramekin or custard cup for each serving and one whole egg in each. Cover with the sauce. Decorate with tarragon or watercress leaves and serve warm.

Cassolettes d'Oeufs aux Champignons
Egg Casseroles with Mushrooms

mushrooms (about ¾ lb for 6 people)   parsley
eggs (one egg per serving)   individual casserole molds
Bechamel Sauce (see *Sauces*)

Wash and blanch mushrooms with enough lemon water to cover them (if mushrooms are nice and white it is not necessary to peel them). Boil for about half a minute. Strain and save water. Chop or grind mushrooms fine. Boil whole eggs for about five minutes, put in cold water and shell without breaking.

Make 1½ cups Bechamel sauce. Add mushrooms and keep hot — add a little of the lemon water to thin the sauce. At the very last minute add 1 egg yolk diluted with a little cream.

Have individual casserole dishes, one per serving, and eggs warm. Put a little of the hot mushroom mixture into the bottom of each dish and on top of this put the egg, and cover with the rest of the mushroom mixture. Sprinkle with parsley or paprika and serve.

Fromage Blanc   Cream Cheese

1 gallon whole milk   dash salt
3 tbsps yogurt or   2 tbsps sweet or sour cream
  1 cup buttermilk

Warm milk slightly. Put buttermilk or yogurt and salt into a large bowl and add the whole milk. Stir and set aside, covered with a plate or plastic bag for 24 hours. It is ready when tested with a spoon, and found to have formed firm curds. Pour thickened mixture into a clean towel, tie up with a string, and hang it on a cabinet or drawer handle. Place a bowl beneath it to catch the drippings. When all of the water has drained from it, remove cheese to a bowl and beat it with a hand beater, adding a little sweet or sour cream, until smooth. Shape it and serve with sugar, strawberries, and sour cream. Use it as you would cream cheese.

VARIATION: Fromage Blanc aux Herbes
Cream Cheese with Herbs
Same as above with the addition of about 2 tbsps of **fines herbes:** tarragon, chervil, chives, parsley, basil. Serve chilled with sliced toasted bread and celery stalks.

L'Omelette Simple   The Plain Omelet

The omelet is the triumph of the egg, according to the poets. It is the dish of improvisation and last-minute preparation. As simple as it is to make an omelet, many do not know the proper procedure. Here are a few observations on making the omelet.

The flame must be fairly high. Use two tbsps of butter for two eggs, beating the eggs moderately just before adding to the pan. Do not stir the eggs while cooking, but rather shake the pan to insure that the eggs do not stick to the pan. Tip pan so egg in the center runs to the sides, then fold it over and with one quick movement, turn it upside down in a warmed dish. "Baveuse" means moist or mellow, and it is the consistency an omelet should be. Do not make them too dry or too drooling.

An omelet is still considered "plain" if it has fine herbs, mushrooms and other vegetables added to it. There are also "les Omelettes Pourrées" or filled omelets, which are always filled before being folded.

Omelette aux Fines Herbes   Fine Herbs Omelet

2 eggs per serving
½ tsp parsley, equal amount of tarragon, chervil, chives, and sweet basil when available and *fresh*. (Same amount of sorrel, lettuce, watercress, but these three particular herbs are optional.)
2 tbsps butter or ¼ stick of butter, for each serving, salt and pepper.

Beat eggs until the whites and yolks are mixed, add salt, pepper and all herbs chopped fine. Follow omelet directions.

Note: Omelettes aux fines herbs should contain what the name implies — fine herbs, namely tarragon, chervil, parsley, chives or spring onions, sweet basil and the optional herbs. It should be enough to make the omelette green and taste like the herbs it contains.

Omelette Pavillon   Omelet with Creamed Chicken
6 servings

2 large fresh tomatoes
12 eggs (2 per serving)
salt and pepper
oregano, thyme
¼ lb mushrooms
garlic, parsley
¼ cup butter or margerine
⅓ cup flour

1½ cups warm milk
salt, pepper and nutmeg
1 shallot or onion
½ lb leftover chicken
½ cup sherry
1 egg yolk
½ cup grated cheese
   (Parmesan or other)

Peel and chop tomatoes, cook in butter with salt, pepper, oregano and thyme. *Strain.* Wash mushrooms, chop and sauté in butter with a small piece of garlic and parsley. Set aside.

Melt butter in double boiler, add flour, stir a minute, add warm milk, stir until smooth, cook 15 to 20 minutes over double boiler, season with salt,

Continued

pepper, nutmeg.

In a separate pot, sauté chopped onion until translucent, but not brown; add chicken, a little of the sauce, and sherry to moisten. To remaining sauce, add egg yolk, diluted with cream and cheese; set aside. Add 2 tbsps of tomato mixture to the beaten eggs, salt, pepper. Make omelet in the usual manner; fold chicken mixture in center, place in baking dish; cover with sauce. Sprinkle with more cheese. Put under broiler and serve.

Omelette à la Chatelaine

Chestnut Omelet
4 servings

¼ lb chestnuts
8 eggs

Glace de viande, enough to
bind chestnuts

Boil chestnuts for 5 minutes, peel off outer shell, then return for another 5 minutes to boil. Shed remainder of skin and braise them in butter and **glace de viande** until soft. Mash them coarsely, add a little butter and enough **glace de viande** to bind to a thick paste. Make an ordinary omelet with 8 eggs, fill with chestnut purée, fold and top with a ribbon of cream sauce.

Cream Sauce

1½ cups warm cream
¼ cup flour

½ cube butter or margarine

Melt butter in a double boiler. Add flour, the warm cream, salt, pepper and nutmeg to taste.

FISH AND SHELLFISH

Fish and Shellfish

A Word From Charles...

   The night that Josephine proposed to me, she made a beautiful dinner of Filet de Sole à Marguery, served with olives, wine and mushrooms. You would go half nuts eating it. We also had a bottle of wine on the table which at that time was illegal because it was during Prohibition. But pretty soon we were eating and having a good time. I was playing the accordion, and Louis, my Vaudeville partner who played the violin, was there too. We always stayed at Mme. Cotain's when we weren't working the vaudeville circuit. All of a sudden, there was a man at the door ~ a Prohibition officer, intent on taking us to jail. We asked him in, gave him something to eat, and pretty soon he was having a good time too, and left in good spirits (actually, he was quite tipsy when he departed).
   After dinner Josephine proposed to me and I said "yes" right away. I didn't stop to think, and yet here we are today, still happy together. We have had a wonderful married life. We were married two weeks later on October 4, 1925 by Father Lebihan at Notre Dame des Victoires. Josephine's cooked for the French Father in her spare time ever since ~ more than fifty years.

 HINT:

The French have made an art of preparing and saucing fish. Poaching in court bouillon is usually done in the oven and is the best way to cook fish evenly. The cooking juices are then thickened or simply added to a Bechamel, Veloute or butter sauce. Any white-fleshed fish can be substituted for the sole.

Filet de Sole Marguery

Sole with Shellfish

1 sole filet for each serving	¼ lb shrimp
1 lb mussels or clams	¼ lb mushrooms
2 shallots	parsley
court bouillon	salt and pepper

Chop shallots and a handful of parsley and the stems of the mushrooms. Lay the filets out flat and spread them with this mixture, add salt and pepper, then roll and fasten them with a toothpick.

Court Bouillon: 1 glass white wine, 1 small carrot, 1 onion, the green of a leek and a few leaves of celery top, thyme, cloves, bay leaves, salt and pepper, 2 cups of fish stock, or any good stock — cook it slowly for ½ hour. *Let it cool.*

Pour the cold cooked court bouillon over the sole and bake in the oven at 350⁰ to 375⁰, for about 10 to 15 minutes.

Prepare a garniture of shrimps, mussels or clams and mushrooms by sautéeing all together.

Place the fish around the edges and the garniture in the center. Pour Sauce Marguery over all; sprinkle with parsley.

Sauce Marguery: Drain juice from sole and keep it warm. Put juice in double boiler, work some butter into flour and drop it in the sauce. Taste for seasoning. Add one egg yolk with ¼ cup cream and pour it over fish.

Filet de Sole Chauchat

Sole with Marnay Sauce
4 to 6 servings

1 cup Bechamel Sauce	1 carrot,
(see Sauces)	1 rib celery
parsley	1 small onion
thyme	1 glass dry white wine
bayleaf	¼ cup grated cheese
6 filets of sole	1 lb potatoes

Boil potatoes and slice. Dice carrot, celery and onion. Make a Bechamel Sauce. In the meantime, salt and pepper the fish filets, sprinkle with parsley; butter a fireproof dish, arrange fish filets in bottom, add vegetables and herbs and pour over a glass of dry white wine. Poach in oven at 375⁰ for 25 to 30 minutes. Take out fish, add liquid to Bechamel Sauce and stir. Add cheese and stir, then line bottom of pan with some of the sauce. On top of this add the sliced potatoes. On the potatoes lay the poached fish, then cover the whole thing with remaining sauce; sprinkle with grated cheese. Put back in oven until browned. Serve in same dish, hot.

Filet de Sole Florentine

Sole with Spinach and Wine
6 servings

2 lbs spinach, washed
Court Bouillon:
  ½ cup water
  ½ cup red wine
1 small onion, sliced
½ carrot, sliced
2 cloves
1 sprig of thyme

1 bay leaf
2 tbsps butter
salt, pepper and nutmeg to taste
6 filets of sole
1 cup sour cream
¼ cup Gruyere or Parmesan
  cheese, grated

Preheat oven to 350⁰.

Cook spinach in very little water for 5 to 7 minutes and drain (or cook in red wine and reserve juices).

To the court bouillon add onions, carrot, cloves and herbs (along with reserved juice of spinach, if any). Simmer very slowly for 15 to 20 minutes and reduce liquid to about ½ cup. Strain.

Chop spinach and then flavor with butter, salt, pepper and nutmeg. Spread evenly over bottom of a buttered fireproof dish.

Arrange filets, folded in half, on top of spinach, pour on the reduced court bouillon and cover with sour cream. Sprinkle with cheese and bake in middle of preheated oven for 15 to 20 minutes until bubbling and the cheese is light brown.

Serve very hot with steamed parsley potatoes.

Filet de Sole au Fromage

Filet of Sole with Cheese
6 servings

6 filets of sole
4 to 6 ozs cheese (Roquefort
  preferred but any
  soft cheese is good)
½ lb butter
1 tsp parsley, chopped
1 tsp chives, chopped

1 shallot, chopped
2 shakes worcestershire
dash of cayenne pepper
salt and pepper
1 egg, beaten slightly
enough flour and bread crumbs
  in which to roll fish

Preheat oven to 375⁰.

Combine cheese, butter, seasonings and herbs together, then spread mixture evenly on sole. Roll filets like sausages and tie securely with string or fasten with toothpicks. To set the butter and cheese mixture, refrigerate the fish until cold. When ready to cook, roll filets first in flour, then egg, and finally in bread crumbs. Arrange them side by side in a buttered fireproof dish. Bake in middle of preheated oven for 15 to 20 minutes. The sole should be brown and crispy. If desired, serve with a Veloute fish sauce (see Sauces).

Tourte aux Fruits de Mer

Fruits of the Sea Pie
8 servings

1 recipe puff paste or
  pâte brisée (see Pastry)
1 to 2 shallots
½ lb mussels (optional)
¼ lb crab
¼ lb shrimp
¼ lb salmon or other fish
2 eggs, beaten

½ cup melted butter
¼ cup flour
½ cup fish fumet (stock), warmed
½ cup white wine
salt and pepper
parsley, nutmeg
1 cup heavy cream
$^1/_3$ cup sherry

Roll puff paste, reserving $^1/_3$ for top. Line a pie platter 9″ to 10″ in diameter according to number of servings, cover and let it rest until ready to use.

Chop shallots and sauté in butter until translucent, add shell fish and sauté lightly in same butter.

Make a fish Veloute with ½ cup melted butter in double boiler, add flour, letting it cook in butter for a couple of minutes. Add the warm fish stock and wine, the salt, pepper, nutmeg to taste, and let cook 15 minutes in double boiler. Off the fire, add the cream, the eggs and sherry. Taste for seasoning; then add all the fish.

Fill the pie dough with the mixture, cover with the rest of the rolled pie dough, glacé with one beaten egg and 1 tbsp of cream. With the remainder of the dough you can decorate the pie with cutout designs, such as a leaf, crescents or other designs of your own. Glacé again and bake at 375⁰ for 25 to 30 minutes. Cover with tin foil if top browns too quickly.

Brandade de Morue, Fleurons

Creamed Potatoes and Codfish with Fleurons

1 lb boneless salt cod
½ cup butter
8 tbsps oil
½ to 1 cup cream, heated
1 to 2 garlic cloves,
  chopped fine
salt, pepper and nutmeg
  6 to 8 oz mashed potatoes
  (about 2 medium potatoes)

Court bouillon:
1 sprig thyme
2 bay leaves
1 grated or chopped onion
2 cups cold water

Fleurons: Crescent shaped
  decorations made from any
  paste: pâte feuilletée,
  pâte brisée, etc., or toast

Soak cod in refrigerator for 24 hours, changing water 3 or 4 times. Make a court bouillon by combining ingredients and bringing to a boil. Simmer 20 minutes, strain, and cool. Add cod to cold bouillon, adding more cold water if necessary to cover. Bring to a boil, turn off heat, and let fish cool in the liquid.

Melt ¼ cup butter with 4 tbsps oil in a skillet. Sauté garlic. Remove skin from cod and check for bones. Flake and add to skillet. Mix to coat cod with garlic, oil, and butter. Add to the potatoes and add seasonings to taste.

In an electric mixer or using a blender, add the cod/potato mixture. Use a medium speed. Slowly add ¼ cup melted butter and 4 tbsps oil. Keep mixing until mixture is smooth and free from lumps. Slowly add cream and check seasonings again. Mixture will be thick like mashed potatoes. If too thick, more cream can be added. Serve hot garnished with fleurons.

Fleurons: Using any paste desired, cut a fluted round (any size). Using the edge of the fluted cutter, cut away ¼ of the round. Bake according to the paste used. Toasted or fried bread may also be used.

To serve: place Morue on a heated platter. Decorate, if desired, with olives, radishes, sliced eggs, etc. Sprinkle with chopped parsley. Place fleurons around.

Note: Creamed turnips may be used in place of potatoes.

Filet de Sole Mariette

4 servings

3 cups of Duchess potatoes
  (see Culinary Glossary)
1 oval fireproof dish, large
Mirepoix: carrot, celery,
  onion
4 filets of sole
butter or margarine
¾ cup white wine
salt and pepper

3 egg yolks
3 tbsps of watercress,
  chervil, tarragon
6 tomatoes

pastry bag and fluted tube
  with large openings

First have ready 3 cups of Duchess potatoes, a large round or oval platter (fire-proof). Put Duchess potatoes in a large pastry bag with fluted tube. Make about four ovals, shaped like a Greek cross, so each of the shapes will hold a filet of sole and brown lightly in the oven or under broiler. With the same mixture of potato make also 4 round *croustates* (like a round shell) and brown them a few minutes under the broiler. Set aside and keep warm.

Preheat oven to 350⁰.

Make a *mirepoix* of diced carrots, celery and onions, sauté in butter. Grease a fire-proof dish large enough to hold the filets of sole, lay the mirepoix in the bottom of the dish, a crumpled bay-leaf, and a sprig of thyme. Lay folded filets of sole over this bed and pour over enough white wine to cover bottom of dish (about ¾ cup). Dot filets with butter, salt, pepper; braise in preheated oven for 15 to 20 minutes. Strain juice and keep fish warm.

Put juice of fish in a small double boiler, add the egg yolks, stirring all the time with a wooden spoon or small wire whip, until creamy.

Blanch the herbs for a few minutes in boiling water, and put through strainer, or chop fine, and add to sauce with salt and pepper, and keep warm.

To assemble, set a filet of sole in each of the oval forms of Duchess pota-

Continued

toes. Between, place the rounds (croustades shells) and fill with the sautéed tomatoes. At the last minute, and off heat, add a piece of fresh butter the size of a walnut, pour some sauce over fish, sprinkle with chopped parsley, chives, or tarragon. Serve remaining sauce in sauciere (gravy bowl). Surround with bouquets of watercress or parsley and wedges of lemon. Serve hot.

Praires Farcis   ## Stuffed Clams

4 clams per serving   2 cloves garlic, chopped
¼ cup butter   breadcrumbs
chopped parsley

Preheat oven to 375⁰.
Open the clams by placing them in a pot over medium heat. Discard one of the shells and loosen the clams.
Mix the butter, chopped parsley and garlic and spread it on the reserved shell with the clam. Sprinkle with breadcrumbs. Bake at 375⁰ until hot, about 5 to 7 minutes.

Scallops à la Diable   *(A recipe of M. Pellaprat)*

2 lbs scallops   ½ lb mushrooms, fresh, or
½ onion, chopped, or shallots   1 small can sliced mushrooms
½ cup margarine: ¼ cup for   2 egg yolks
   sautéeing, ¼ cup for sauce   ¼ cup cream
¹/₃ cup sherry, sauterne,   1 to 2 tbsps lemon juice
   'or chablis   bread crumbs
½ tsp dry mustard or   parmesan cheese
1 tsp prepared mustard   scallop shells
salt, pepper and nutmeg   cayenne

Wash and dry scallops, cut in 2 or 3 pieces depending on size. Lightly flour scallops. Sauté chopped onions, or shallots in *clarified* butter; do not brown. In separate pan, sauté sliced mushrooms. Sauté scallops on high heat for 2 minutes after removing onions. Then remove scallops; salt and pepper them. Deglaze pan with sherry or white wine, and return scallops to pan.

Sauce Supreme:
2 tbsps flour   ¹/₃ cup sherry or white wine
¼ cup margarine   ½ tsp dry mustard dissolved
1 cup chicken broth (approx.)   in water
salt, pepper, nutmeg, cayenne   1 tbsp lemon juice (approx.)

Add mushrooms and onions to sauce.

Grease scallop shells generously. Border shells with Duchess potatoes (see below)*. Put a little sauce in each shell. Mix 2 egg yolks with cream, and beat into remaining sauce carefully; add scallops. Fill shells with this mixture. Sprinkle with fine bread crumbs, grated cheese, and dot with margarine to improve browning. *Gratinée.* (If prepared in advance, re-heat in 350° oven.)

Duchess potatoes: Boil, peel, mash 4 baking potatoes. Beat in ¼ cup margarine, 1 tsp salt, pepper, nutmeg (dash). Omit eggs or cream. Put in pastry bag using large star tube for decorating scallop shells.

Note: That Pellaprat's version of duchess potatoes omits eggs, while my own (see Culinary Glossary) includes them.

Langouste en Civet

Lobster Stew

1 rock lobster
2 tbsps oil
¼ cup cognac or brandy
4 tbsps butter
1 medium onion, chopped
2 shallots, chopped
1 carrot, finely chopped
1 clove garlic, minced
1 cup white wine
1 tbsp tomato paste

1 tsp parsley, chopped
1 bay leaf
salt and pepper
pinch of cayenne
2 tbsps **beurre manie**
 (see Sauces)
croutons (French bread slices,
 rubbed with a clove of garlic
 and fried in butter)
parsley to sprinkle on top

Split the lobster in half lengthwise. Cut the tail and claws and remove the head. Slice the body into scallops. Heat the oil in a heavy frying pan large enough to hold the lobster comfortably. Cook the lobster over a brisk heat for about 5 minutes. Pour the cognac over it and ignite.

Heat the butter in a separate sauce pan and sauté the onions, carrot, shallots, and garlic until they are tender, but not brown. Add the vegetables to the lobster. Warm the wine and add, together with the tomato paste, parsley, and bay leaf. Season to taste with salt, pepper, and cayenne. Cover and cook over low heat for about 15 minutes. Take out the lobster pieces and arrange them on a platter. Keep them warm.

Add the **beurre manié** to the sauce, stirring until it is thickened. Bring it almost to a boil, adjust the seasoning, and pour it through a sieve onto the lobster.

Garnish with croutons and sprinkle with parsley.

Quiche au Crabe

Crab Quiche with Mushrooms
6 to 8 servings

Bechamel Sauce: (see Sauces)
½ lb butter
4 eggs, beaten
$^1/_3$ cup cognac
$^1/_3$ cup sour cream
1 clove garlic, minced
¼ lb mushrooms, coarse chopped
1 prebaked 9″ x 13″ pastry shell

½ lb crab, flaked
1 shallot, chopped
$^1/_3$ cup Parmesan cheese (grated)
½ cup white wine
fresh herbs, chopped:
    1 tbsp fines herbes (see Glossary)
    1 tsp aromatic herbs (see Glossary)

Prepare Bechamel. Let cook at least 25 minutes. Meanwhile, melt 1 to 1½ tbsps butter and sauté shallot. Pour in the wine and ignite. Stir into Bechamel. Melt 2 to 3 tbsps butter and sauté the crab. Pour in the cognac and ignite. Add to the Bechamel along with the herbs, sour cream, eggs, and cheese. Now melt 4 tbsps of butter. When very hot, sauté the mushrooms. Add the garlic and stir into the egg mixture. Pour into the pre-baked shell and loosely cover with tin foil. Bake in a 375⁰ oven for 30 to 35 minutes, or until an inserted knife comes out clean. Uncover last 15 minutes.

Le Saumon en Papillotte
8 servings

Salmon in Parchment

1 whole salmon, boned and
    spread open
Marinade: fennel, dill,
    thyme, bay leaf, chervil
    1 to 2 cups white wine
    1 to 2 tbsps lemon juice
    and/or a few lemon slices
parchment paper, large
    enough to envelop fish

Sauce Beurre Blanc:
    ¼ lb butter
    ¼ cup white wine
    1 to 2 tbsps lemon juice
    3 to 4 shallots, chopped fine
chopped parsley
oil (olive oil preferred)
foil
salt and pepper

Combine ingredients for the marinade and marinate the salmon overnight. Before cooking, remove the fish from the marinade, reserving liquid. Oil the parchment paper and place fish in the center. Rub fish with oil and season with salt and pepper. Strain the marinade and place the herbs on the fish. Envelop fish in the paper and seal package with foil. Place in a shallow pan and bake in a 350⁰ oven for 45 minutes.

To serve: remove fish gently from paper and place on a heated platter. Sprinkle with fresh chopped parsley and Sauce *Beurre Blanc:* Combine the wine, lemon juice, and shallots with the liquid from the marinade. Reduce to 1 to 2 tbsps over high heat. Remove pan from the heat and add the butter, 1 tbsp at a time. Beat with each addition, being careful not to let the butter melt. Season with salt and pepper.

Saumon à l'Aigre-Douce

Sweet and Sour Salmon
8 to 10 servings

1 slice of salmon
  for each serving

Court bouillon (or fish stock,
  if available)
sweet and sour sauce

Court bouillon:
1 cup white wine
½ cup water
2 tbsps vinegar
¼ cup carrot, chopped
¼ cup celery, chopped

¼ cup onion, chopped
2 to 3 cloves
salt and pepper
1 sprig thyme
1 bay leaf

Make a court bouillon with the ingredients listed above or use fish stock, if you have it on hand. Bring the court bouillon or stock to a boil and let it cool. Preheat oven to 325⁰.

Wash the fish and put it in an ovenproof dish. Pour the court bouillon over the fish and cover, first with waxed paper and then with aluminum foil. Bake at 325⁰ for 20 to 25 minutes, until just done. Do not overcook. Let the fish cool in the court bouillon. Serve cold with Sauce Aigre-Douce (sweet and sour sauce).

Sauce Aigre-Douce

Sweet and Sour Sauce for Fish
Makes about 1½ cups

1 cup maple syrup
½ cup vinegar
½ cup wine (or water)
1 onion, chopped
12 lemon slices
1 apple, cored and diced

1 tbsp raisins
1 pinch cloves
1 tbsp fennel leaves,
  chopped
salt and pepper
almonds for decoration

Put the syrup, vinegar and wine (or water) in a quart saucepan and add the chopped onion, lemon slices, diced apple, raisins and the spices. Let the sauce come to a full boil, cover and simmer until the lemon slices and apple are glazed.

Pour the sauce over fish and decorate with almonds.

Escargots de Bourgogne

Burgundy Snails

6 snails per serving

Burgundy butter *(below)*

Prepare the snail butter. Put a little of the butter in the bottom of each

Continued

snail shell. Put in a snail and a little more butter.

Set the shells on a dish especially made for snails or put rock salt in a pan to steady the shells. Heat in a 400° oven for 10 minutes until the butter is bubbling.

Beurre d'Escargot: Snail Butter

Chop 3 tbsps parsley and 2 cloves garlic very fine and mix with ¾ lb soft butter to make a smooth paste. Add ½ tsp salt and ¾ tsp pepper. Chill until ready to use.

Colin à la Russe   Chilled Fish with Vegetables

1 center cut from whole fish
  (weight according to how
  many being served)
cooked vegetables:
  beans, carrots, turnips, etc.
salt and pepper
1 cup mayonnaise (see Sauces)
2 cups clarified fish stock,
  chicken stock, or beef stock

1 to 2 tbsps chopped fresh herbs:
  fennel, thyme, marjoram
½ cup fish stock
chopped olives
1 tbsp gelatin plus 1 tsp
French dressing to marinate
  vegetables (see Sauces)
3 to 4 hard-boiled eggs

Season fish cavity with salt, pepper and the chopped herbs. Place in oven-proof dish (with a tight-fitting lid) or fish poacher. Add fish stock and bring to a boil on top of the stove. Grease a piece of waxed paper and place over the fish before covering with lid. Place in a preheated 375° oven for 10 to 15 minutes (depending on size of fish). Cool.

Cube cooked vegetables and marinate in French dressing. Separate whites from the yolks of the eggs and press both whites and yolks (separately) through a sieve. Set aside.

Soften 1 tsp gelatin in cold water in a custard cup or other heat resistant container. Place cup in hot water, stirring if necessary, until gelatin is completely dissolved. Stir into mayonnaise. Working quickly, coat the cool fish piece with the jellied mayonnaise. Set into refrigerator to cool.

Soften 1 tbsp gelatin in cold water before adding it to the clarified stock. Heat and stir until gelatin is completely dissolved. Let stock cool, but not too cold as it will quickly jell. Place fish piece at end of an oval platter, being careful not to disturb the jellied mayonnaise. Decorate fish piece with pimentos, green part of scallions, sliced olives, or whatever if desired. Quickly spoon stock over.

Place the marinated vegetables next to the fish, shaping opposite end to a point. Place sieved yolks over one half of the vegetable, pressing them in place. Do the same with the whites over the other half. Leave a strip of vegetables between the whites and yolks. Press chopped olives over this space. Spoon remaining jellied stock over vegetables if desired. Serve with a seasoned mayonnaise.

Mousse de Sole Amandine

Sole Amandine Mousse
4 to 6 servings

Most often fish mousses are served cold. Here's one that is served warm. The mushroom-almond sauce adds a crunchy texture contrast to the mousse.

1 lb filet of sole
2 tbsps cornstarch
1 cup heavy cream
¾ tsp ground sage
⅓ cup finely-chopped
   green onion

¼ cup slivered almonds
3 eggs, separated
1½ tsp salt
¼ tsp pepper
Mushroom-Almond Sauce *(below)*

Place fish in freezer until it is nearly frozen. Cut into small squares; place in electric blender, ¹/₃ at a time, and process until fish is finely chopped. Mix fish with almonds, cornstarch, egg yolks, cream, salt, sage, pepper and green onion.

Whip egg whites until stiff and fold into fish mixture. Turn into well-buttered 5½ or 6-cup casserole or soufflé dish. Place in pan with hot water in bottom; bake in a 350⁰ oven for 45 minutes or until a pick inserted into center comes out dry. Serve hot with Mushroom-Almond Sauce.

Mushroom-Almond Sauce

¹/₃ cup slivered almonds
1 10¾ oz can condensed
   cream of mushroom soup

1 tbsp butter or margarine
½ cup dry white wine
1 tbsp finely-chopped
   fresh chives

Sauté almonds in butter in skillet until golden. Mix in undiluted soup, wine and chives. Heat through.

Quenelles

Fish Dumplings

1 recipe pâte à choux
   (see Pastry Dough)
1¼ lbs skinless, boneless fish
   (Halibut, whiting, sole, cod,
   or flounder. Pike is best, if
   available.)

⅛ tsp nutmeg
½ tsp salt
¼ tsp white pepper
2 to 6 tbsp chilled
   whipping cream

Continued

Follow the recipe for pâte à choux, using 2 eggs and 2 additional egg whites.

The fish should be ground very fine. 1¼ lb of fish should yield about 2 cups. Beat in an equal amount of pâte à choux and the salt, pepper, and nutmeg. Cool the mixture in the refrigerator until well chilled.

Just before you are ready to make the quenelles, bring a large saucepan of water to the boiling point and beat the cream into the mixture by the spoonful until it is firm enough to hold its shape in a wooden spoon. (Too much cream will make the quenelles too soft, so it is best to test one in the barely simmering water.)

Form the quenelles with two spoons, as described below, which will make them very light in texture, or by rolling them in flour and shaping them into cylinders (these will not be so light and delicate).

Two spoon method of shaping: Set out two dessert size spoons in a glass of water. With a wet spoon dip out a spoonful of cold quenelle paste and smooth the top with the second wet spoon. Then slip the spoon from under the quenelle and drop it in the simmering water. Form the rest of the quenelles the same way, as quickly as possible. Poach them uncovered for 10 to 15 minutes. Do NOT allow the water to boil. The quenelles are done when they have doubled in size and roll over easily.

Remove with slotted spoon and dry on a towel. Serve with Mousseline Sauce, drawn butter or Bechamel Sauce, sprinkled with cheese and **gratinee.**

Note: If the quenelles are not to be served immediately, arrange them on a lightly buttered dish and brush them with melted butter; cover with plastic wrap and refrigerate. They will keep at least two days.

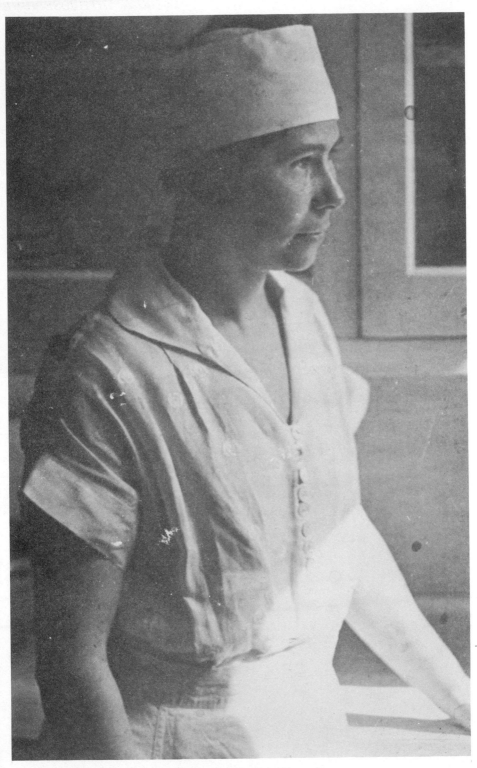

A much younger me ~ newly-arrived in San Francisco

Charles, on the Orpheum Circuit

Charles and I in our kitchen

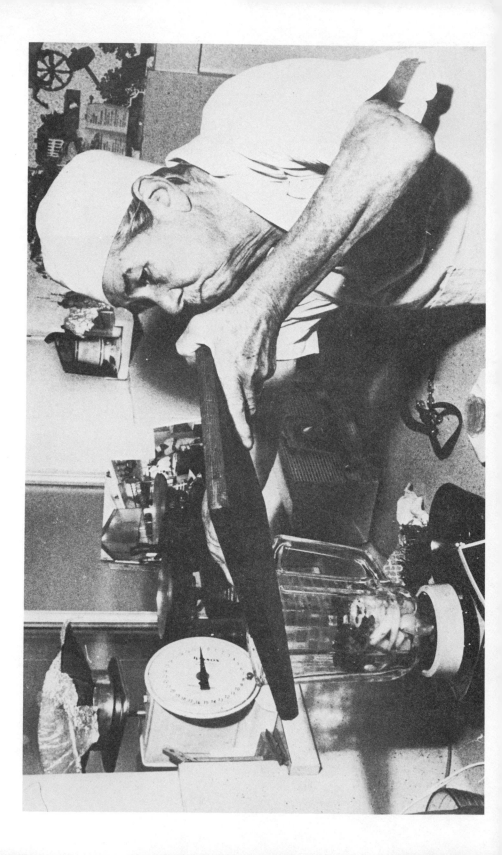

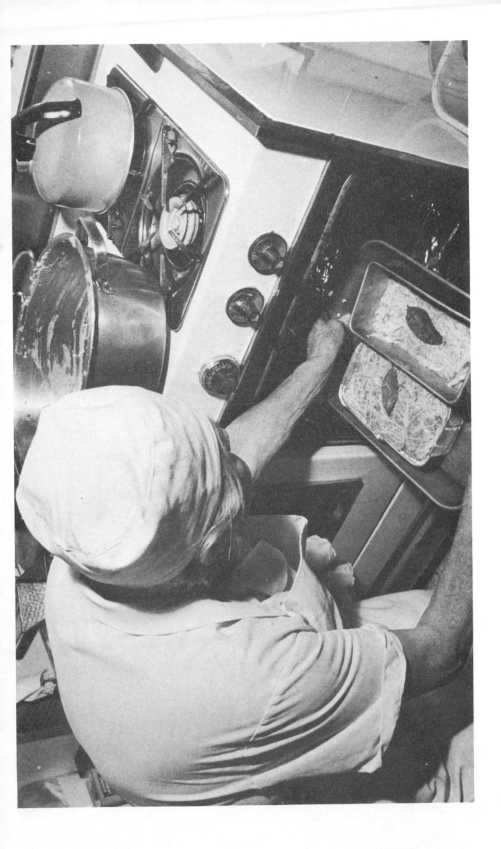

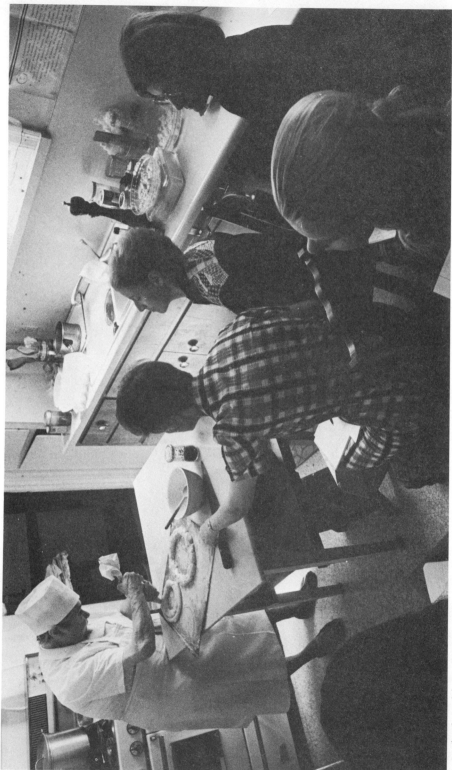

A typical cooking class

CHICKEN, TURKEY, PIGEON, DUCK, PHEASANT, RABBIT

My second Cordon-Bleu diploma

Chicken, Turkey, Pigeon, Duck, Pheasant, Rabbit

The Cordon Bleu that I attended was quite different from the one of today. It stressed the fundamentals of cooking. We learned how to make all of the sauces, pastes, soups, and all of the other basics. Only then were we taught the haute cuisine.

When I entered the school I was twenty-two years old. I had just left the convent and begun work for the Louis Loucheur family. They paid for my tuition at the Cordon Bleu, which is why I was able to go for four years. Classes were held in two locations: in the morning I went to the Rue de la Pompe for two hours to learn the fundamentals, and in the afternoon I spent two hours at the Fauberg Saint Honoré where more elaborate dishes were prepared. My day was a long one, since I had to prepare all the meals for the Loucheur family ~ but I was young, very happy, and filled with a love of God and the world He made. I went to mass every morning, before the household woke up ~ and I still go to daily mass today.

My teacher was the great chef, Henri-Paul Pellaprat. He was a wonderful man, very jolly and patient with his students. We would watch him cook, and when he was finished, he would always answer any questions. Sometimes he would call one of us to the stove to assist him, and that was a privilege. I helped him often, because he said I was a natural cook. When I was not busy at the Loucheurs, I would go to his house in La Varenne, to help him with his dinner parties. I learned more from him there than I did in class. I remember once at his house, one of his beautiful creations was dropped on the floor just before it was to be served. Pellaprat was very calm; he turned to me and asked me to help him repair the damage. The dish was served and was a success, naturally. Afterward, he said, "Little did they know what went on in the kitchen!" He had an excellent sense of humor.

I received my first diploma from the Cordon Bleu in 1923. When I left, Pellaprat placed the toque blanche, the mark of a chef, on my head, and declared, "I crown you chef."

NOTE: Josephine received a second diploma in 1927 when she returned to Paris with Mrs. George Oppen, and completed a six-month course in Pastries and Desserts. Josephine kept in touch with Pallaprat over the years, through correspondence and visits, until his death in 1948. Of the recipes he gave to her, some appear in print here for the first time.

HINT: Clarification du Beurre (Clarified Butter)

This is done by heating the butter over a very gentle fire. The butter melts and appears as clear as olive oil. When the "residue" forms a whitish deposit in the bottom of the pan, decant and strain off the clear butter into another receptacle. It will keep a very long time without getting rancid. The residue does not have to be thrown away; it is good to flavor vegetables and soups.

Suprême Marie Thérèse

Chicken Breasts with Chestnuts

4 servings

4 whole chicken breasts, boned
salt and pepper
½ cup cream cheese (homemade or
    store bought)
½ cup soft cheese: Brie, Camembert,
    Boursin, etc.
2 tbsps fresh herbs, chopped:
    1½ tbsps fine herbs: tarragon,
    parsley, chervil
    ½ tbsp aromatic herbs: rosemary,
    thyme, bay leaf, oregano,
    marjoram, etc.
Sauce Marron (below)

6 to 8 slices Prosciutto
½ cup chestnut purée (chestnuts puréed
    with a little milk)
Caul from pork
    (or cheesecloth)
4 tbsps butter
2 tbsps oil
Mirepoix: 1 stalk celery,
    1 carrot, 1 onion or white part of
    leek, 1 cup deglazing liquid:
    wine and/or stock
parsley, chopped

Preheat oven to 375°.

Salt and pepper the chicken breasts. Combine the cream cheese with the soft cheese and mix in the herbs. Spread this mixture over the chicken breasts. Lay the Prosciutto slices over the cheese, trimming to fit. Now spread purée of chestnuts over the ham. Fold the breast over and wrap in the caul or cheesecloth.

Melt the butter with the oil and brown the chicken breasts. Remove to an oven-proof casserole that has a tight-fitting lid. Chop the **Mirepoix** and sauté in the same pan in which the chicken was browned. Deglaze the pan with the wine and stock, being sure to scrape up any bits that may stick to the bottom of the pan. Pour the juices over the chicken, cover, and cook in preheated oven for 30 minutes.

Ingredients for Sauce Marron:
3 tbsps butter
1 or 2 shallots, chopped fine
3 tbsps flour

1½ cups **fond blanc,** warmed
1 tbsp chopped herbs (same as above)
½ cup cooked chestnuts, chopped

Prepare the sauce by melting the butter in the top of a double boiler over medium heat. Sauté the shallots and add the flour. Slowly add the **fond blanc**. Stir in the herbs and chopped chestnuts.

When the chicken has finished cooking, remove the breasts to a warm platter and add the cooking juices to the sauce, being careful not to thin the sauce too much. Pour the sauce over the chicken breasts and sprinkle with some chopped parsley before serving.

Cuisse de Poulet Farcies

Stuffed Chicken Thighs
Makes 18 stuffed thighs

18 chicken thighs, boned and
   flattened slightly
Filling:
½ lb raw chicken
½ lb pork sausage
¼ lb blood sausage, cooked
¼ lb chicken livers, poached
   for a few minutes
1 onion
2 tbsps chopped parsley
1 tbsp chives
1 clove garlic
1 sprig fresh thyme
1 egg
2 pieces of bread, soaked in milk
   or bouillon and squeezed dry
salt and pepper

Caul or fat back, cut in strips
clarified butter, oil, or bacon
   fat to brown the chicken
½ cup brandy
1 shallot
2 sprigs thyme
1 bay leaf
1 clove garlic
1 onion, chopped fine
1 tbsp flour
1½ cups white wine
1½ cups chicken broth

Grind together all the ingredients listed under filling, except the egg and bread. Mix in the egg and bread and season with salt and pepper. Place one to two tablespoons of the filling in the center of each thigh and roll closed, securing with caul or fat back pulled tightly around each piece of meat.

Brown on all sides in hot fat and season with salt and pepper. Drain off the fat (it may be necessary to remove the thighs to do this). Return thighs to pan and pour in the brandy. Ignite. When the flame dies, add the shallots, thyme, bay leaf, garlic, onion, flour, wine, and broth. Bring to a boil. Cover and continue cooking over medium heat (or bake in a preheated 350° oven) for 25 to 30 minutes.

Poulet Amandine

Chicken with Almonds
6 servings

1 chicken (4 to 5 lbs), cut up
½ cup butter
1 small onion, chopped
1 clove garlic, chopped
⅓ cup sherry
3 small tomatoes, seeded
  and chopped
3 tbsps flour

1 tbsp tomato paste
½ cup almonds, grated
1 bay leaf
salt and pepper to taste
1½ cups chicken broth
½ cup sour cream
2 tbsps Swiss cheese, grated
Parmesan cheese, grated

Preheat oven to 350⁰.
Fry the chicken on all sides in butter, then remove from the pan and set aside. In the same butter sauté the onions and garlic until transparent. Then add the sherry and tomatoes. Cook the mixture until light brown. Mix in the flour and tomato paste and stir well. Add almonds, bay leaf, and salt and pepper.

Place the chicken in an oven-proof dish, add the chicken broth and top with the sauce. Bake in preheated oven for 45 minutes.

When chicken is cooked, remove and keep warm. On top of the stove reduce the juices a little, then add 1 tbsp of the sour cream and 2 tbsps Swiss cheese. Bring quickly to a boil. Return the chicken to the casserole, top with dollops of remaining sour cream and sprinkle with Parmesan cheese. Place under the broiler for a few seconds to brown the top.

Poulet aux Coings

Chicken with Quinces
8 servings

1 chicken, about 3 to 4 lbs
¼ cup butter
3 tbsps oil
1 lb onions, peeled and chopped
1 tbsp coriander leaves, chopped
1 tbsp paprika

1 tbsp fresh ginger (or ½ tsp powdered)
1 pinch saffron
salt and pepper to taste
1½ cups broth (beef or chicken)
4 quinces (½ quince per serving)
2 tbsps each butter and oil
parsley

Cut the chicken in pieces and sauté them in half the butter and oil until golden brown on all sides. Take them out and set aside. Sauté the onions in the same fat and allow to cook slowly for 10 minutes, stirring often. Preheat oven to 375⁰.

Put the chicken and onions in a casserole and add the coriander leaves, the paprika, ginger, saffron, and salt and pepper to taste. *Deglaze* the pan with 1½ cups of chicken or beef broth, scraping up the bits from the pan. Pour into the casserole, over the chicken pieces. Set aside.

Peel the quinces, cut in two, take out the seeds, wash and dry them and sauté in 2 tbsps of butter and 2 tbsps oil (or more if needed). Brown the quinces until they almost caramelize. Put the sautéed quinces on top of the chicken in the casserole, cover, and bake in the oven at 375⁰ or cook on top of the stove over very low heat for 30 to 45 minutes.

Set half a quince for each serving around the platter and put the chicken in the center. Pour the juice over and sprinkle with parsley. Serve with rice.

Poulet Sauté à la Choucroute   ## Chicken and Sauerkraut
4 to 5 servings

1 ½ lbs sauerkraut, for chicken
additional sauerkraut for serving
1 fryer (3 to 4 lbs), cut up
7 tbsps bacon fat or shortening
½ cup onions, finely chopped

2 cloves garlic, minced
1 tbsp finely chopped hot
   chili peppers
salt and pepper
½ cup chicken stock

Preheat oven to 300⁰.

Wash and soak the sauerkraut for 10 to 20 minutes and squeeze dry. Brown the chicken pieces, skin side first then turn, in 4 tbsps hot fat. Set them aside. Add the rest of the fat to the pan, and when hot, add the onions and garlic and cook for 2 to 3 minutes. Add the 1 ½ lbs sauerkraut, the chili peppers, and freshly ground black pepper to taste. Cook uncovered for 10 minutes over medium heat. Lay the pieces of chicken on top and pour the chicken stock over. Cover and bake in a preheated oven for 30 minutes.

Serve on a bed of sauerkraut or surrounded by additional sauerkraut.

Poulet Champenoise   ## Chicken Champenoise
6 to 8 servings

2 chickens, 2 to 3 lbs each, either
   broilers or fryers, cut in pieces
¼ cup brandy or cognac
2 oz butter or margarine
1 package dried mushrooms (1 oz)
1 large onion (chopped)
1 clove garlic
⅓ cup flour

¼ cup catsup
2 cups chicken or veal broth
1 cup heavy cream
1 pinch cayenne
2 tbsps tarragon vinegar
¼ lb fresh mushrooms, thinly sliced
½ bottle champagne or dry white wine
tarragon leaves
Glace de viande, or a little beef extract

Soak dried mushrooms in water, drain and chop finely. Pat chicken dry with paper towels and remove skin if desired. Heat 2 tbsps of butter and one of oil, brown chicken, a few pieces at a time, on all sides, adding more butter if needed and removing chicken as it is browned.

Put chicken in Dutch oven. In a small saucepan, heat brandy slightly, pour over chicken and ignite with a match. When the flame dies, remove chicken.

To pan juices add dried mushrooms, onion and garlic. Cook over low heat a

Continued

few minutes, then remove from heat, and stir in flour, catsup, cayenne until well blended. Gradually stir in chicken broth and ⅓ cup of cream and bring to a boil, stirring.

Return chicken to Dutch oven, add tarragon leaves, sliced fresh mushrooms and **glace de viande.** Simmer covered for 40 to 45 minutes. Remove chicken.

Stir cream, vinegar and champagne into sauce in Dutch oven and simmer five minutes. Remove from heat and serve with chicken.

Poulet Sauté Singapore

Braised Chicken Singapore
4 servings

1 large fryer, cut up	chopped parsley
flour	bay leaf
¼ cup butter, 1 tbsp oil	thyme and tarragon
salt and pepper	¼ cup white wine
1 large onion, chopped	¼ cup chicken broth
2 cloves garlic, minced	1 tsp curry powder

Preheat oven to 350⁰.

Roll the pieces of chicken in flour and sauté them in the butter until they are golden brown. Transfer them to a fireproof casserole and sprinkle them with salt and pepper. Sauté the onions and garlic and add to the chicken, along with the herbs. Deglaze the pan with the white wine and chicken broth, scraping all the brown crust from sides of the pan, and pour over the chicken. Sprinkle with the curry powder. Cover and bake 45 minutes in a preheated oven.

Serve with rice.

Poulet de Grains Henri Pellaprat

Young Broilers
Henri Pellaprat
6 servings

1 lb onions, sliced	1 tbsp tomato paste
¼ cup butter	1 tsp curry powder
2 tbsps oil	1 tsp paprika
3 young broilers, halved	juice of 1 lemon
2 oz cognac	¼ lb mushrooms, sautéed
½ cup chablis or sautern	1 truffle (optional)
½ pint heavy cream	salt and pepper to taste
1 cup Bechamel sauce (see *Sauces*)	chopped parsley

Sauté the onions until translucent in the butter and oil. Remove the onions from the pan and sauté the chicken in the same oil. (Or the chicken may be brushed with butter and oil and broiled until a light golden brown.) Return the onions to the pan with the chicken, pour the cognac over and ignite. Add the wine and cook until slightly reduced. Add the cream and cook over medium heat for 20 to 25 minutes.

Remove the chicken and add the Bechamel sauce and tomato paste to the onions. Put the entire mixture through a fine sieve or purée in a blender. Return to a pan and let it come to a boil over medium heat. Add the curry powder, paprika, and lemon juice. Stir thoroughly and add the sautéed mushrooms and chicken. Simmer 10 minutes.

Remove the chicken to a hot platter, spoon the sauce over it and sprinkle with parsley. Garnish with a truffle if desired.

 HINT: Truffles

Fresh truffles can be kept only if stored in alcohol. Josephine keeps them in brandy or sherry.

Poulet à la Flamande Farci

Chicken Stuffed with Cream Cheese

1 good-sized chicken
chicken fat or oil
16 oz cream cheese
1 whole egg
herbs: 2 tbsps chives, chopped
    2 tbsps chopped parsley
    2 tbsps tarragon, chopped
    few thyme and oregano leaves,
      chopped

salt and pepper
¼ tsp nutmeg
2 egg yolks
crème fraîche (see below)

Preheat oven to 375°.

Melt chicken fat in a heavy skillet with a tight fitting lid. Mix cream cheese with the whole egg and chopped herbs. Season with salt, pepper and ¼ tsp nutmeg. Season cavity with salt and pepper and stuff with the cream cheese mixture. Tie chicken securely and brown well on all sides in the chicken fat. Season generously with salt and pepper, cover, and bake for 30 to 45 minutes, until juices run clear, in a preheated oven.

Mix yolks with the crème fraîche and add ½ tsp nutmeg. When chicken has finished cooking, remove from pan and spoon off fat. To the pan juices, add the crème fraîche mixture and heat through, scraping off the bits from the bottom of the pan. Carve chicken and spoon sauce over. Sprinkle with chopped parsley and serve.

Crème Fraîche:

Stir 2 tbsps sour cream or buttermilk into 1 cup heavy (whipping) cream. Let stand at room temperature for 24 hours. If very warm, refrigerate after 12 hours. Keeps 10 days to two weeks refrigerated.

Poulet aux Crevettes

Roast Chicken Stuffed with Shrimp
4 servings

1 chicken (4½ to 5 lbs)
½ tsp marjoram (⅛ tsp if dry)
1 tsp salt
6 to 8 slices white bread, stale
1 cup heavy cream
4 tbsps butter, melted
2 egg yolks
8 large shrimp, cooked and
  coarsely chopped

4 large shrimp, uncooked and finely
  chopped or puréed in a blender
½ cup parsley, finely chopped
¼ cup cooked peas
½ tsp salt
freshly ground black pepper, to taste
2 egg whites
½ cup butter, melted

Preheat oven to 350°.

Rub the inside of the chicken with salt and marjoram. Toast the bread on a rack in the upper third of the oven until it is dried but not brown. Crumble it and soak it in the cream in a saucepan for about 5 minutes. Add 4 tbsps melted butter and cook over low heat, stirring constantly, until the mixture is pasty and smooth, resembling a soft dough. Remove it from the heat and cool for about 10 minutes; then beat in the yolks, one at a time, beating well each time. Beat in the cooked shrimp, the raw shrimp, parsley and peas. Add the salt and pepper. Beat the egg whites until stiff and fold them into the stuffing.

Fill the breast cavity of the chicken, but do not pack it tightly because the stuffing will expand as it cooks. Fold the neck skin under the chicken and secure with a skewer or thread. Stuff the body cavity loosely (not more than ¼ full) and close with skewers, thread, or trussing pins.

Brush a little melted butter over the entire chicken and place it on a rack in a roasting pan just large enough to hold it. Pour the rest of the butter over the breast. Roast the chicken in the middle of the oven for about 1½ hours, basting frequently with the pan juices.

Pierce the chicken to test for doneness. If the juices are yellow, the chicken is done. If they are still pink, roast for a few minutes longer. Remove the chicken to a heated serving platter and let it stand about 10 minutes before carving. Dilute the pan juices with chicken stock if desired and bring to a boil. Serve the juices with the chicken.

Poulet à la Mère Fillioux (Lyon)

Chicken Stuffed with Chicken Livers

8 servings

Stuffing:
8 chicken livers
¼ cup butter
salt and pepper
1 small can truffles (optional)
½ cup cream (part for stuffing and part for the sauce)
1 oz brandy

2 young chickens (3 lbs each)
juice of 1 lemon

2 cups dry white wine
1 cup chicken broth
1 large carrot, finely chopped
2 inner stalks of celery, chopped
2 shallots, chopped
1 tbsp chopped parsley
1 tbsp chopped chervil
2 whole cloves
3 egg yolks
coarse salt
cheesecloth

Prepare the liver stuffing: sauté the livers in a little butter and chop very fine. Add the remaining butter to the chopped livers, season with salt and pepper. Add 1 truffle cut in small pieces, a little cream to moisten the mixture, and the brandy.

Rub the skin of the chickens with lemon juice and insert slices of 1 truffle under the skin, being careful not to break the skin. This will flavor the flesh of the chicken.

Pour the wine and broth into a large pot and add the carrot, celery, shallots, parsley, chervil, trimmings of the truffles, and 2 whole cloves.

Divide the liver stuffing into two equal parts and stuff the two chickens. Wrap each bird in a layer of cheesecloth to hold the stuffing in place. Put them on a circular trivet in the pot. Cover the pot with a piece of parchment that has been moistened or tinfoil, to insure an air-tight container. Put on the cover and steam the contents for 45 to 50 minutes. *DO NOT OPEN WHILE COOKING.* The chickens must be almost ready to fall apart when done. Serve with two sauces, as follows.

SAUCES:

Thick Sauce: Drain some liquid out of the pot, leaving the vegetables and enough liquid to serve as the thin sauce. Put the drained liquid in a small saucepan over low heat. Mix the egg yolks with the remaining cream, and add to the liquid, stirring until the sauce thickens. When it coats the spoon, pour it into a warm sauce-boat.

Thin Sauce: Put the rest of the liquid and the vegetables left in the pot into another warm sauce-boat.

Note: Use coarse salt, grinding it in a small grinder. It has a flavor different from "commercial" salt.

Timbale à la Courtisane

Crêpe-Lined Mold Filled with Chicken and Mushrooms
6 to 8 servings

Brittany Crêpes:
3 eggs, beaten
1 cup liquid: half milk,
    half water
3 rounded tbsps buckwheat flour
1 tsp cinnamon
½ tsp salt
2 cups Bechamel sauce
5 medium onions, sliced
1 whole egg
1 lb cooked chicken, chopped fine
    (see *Note*)

2 tbsps butter
½ cup chicken stock or cream (or more)
salt and pepper, to taste
nutmeg, to taste
2 to 3 tbsps butter
¼ lb mushrooms, chopped
3 cloves garlic, chopped fine
2 to 3 tbsps parsley, chopped
3 egg yolks
additional parsley for garnish

Prepare the crêpes, following the method in the basic recipe for crêpes (see *Pastry Dough*). Lightly film a **timbale** or desired mold (large or individual) and line it with crêpes. If using a large mold, place one crêpe on the bottom and line the sides with others, leaving the ends free to overlap over the filling. For smaller molds line with one or more crêpes, depending on size, pressing against the sides. Set the mold aside. Refrigerating it will help hold the crêpes to the side while filling the mold.

Prepare the *Bechamel sauce.*

For **Sauce Soubise,** sauté the onions in a little butter until transparent (do not let them brown). Add a little chicken stock or cream and continue cooking onions, adding more liquid as necessary until the onions are thoroughly cooked. Place 1 cup of Bechamel and 5 tbsps of the onions in a blender and purée. Season with salt, pepper, and nutmeg to taste. Thin the sauce with cream or stock if too thick.

Melt 2 to 3 tbsps butter and sauté the mushrooms. Add the chopped garlic and parsley. Season with salt and pepper. Add the egg and egg yolks to 1 cup of Bechamel and mix well. Combine the mushrooms and chicken with enough Bechamel to moisten the mixture. Taste and adjust the seasoning. Reserve remaining sauce for serving.

Preheat oven to 350°.

Fill the mold, overlapping the ends of the crêpes over it. Place in a **bain-marie.** Bake on the middle shelf of the oven for 20 minutes.

Cover and cook 5 to 10 minutes more, until cooked through (test with a knife — if it comes out clean the **timbale** is done.) Unmold and spoon some **Sauce Soubise** over the **timbale.** Sprinkle with parsley.

Serve the remaining sauce on the side.

Note: Shellfish or veal may be substituted for the chicken.

Poulet Montpelier

Chicken with Herbs and Cheese
8 servings

4 whole chicken breasts, boned
salt and pepper
⅛ tsp each: oregano, marjoram,
  parsley, tarragon, chervil, chives.
  Use fresh if possible.

1 cup sautern or chicken broth
¼ lb cheese, not processed
1 cup flour
2 beaten eggs
1 cup breadcrumbs

Cut breasts in half, making 8 pieces. Remove skin and membranes. Place each piece between waxed paper and flatten with mallet or cleaver to about ⅛ inch thick. Sprinkle with salt and pepper. Set aside. Whip butter until fluffy and stir in herbs. Cut cheese lengthwise into 8 pieces. Spread herb-butter on cheese and on breasts, saving some butter for sauce. Place a stick of cheese on each cutlet and roll up, tucking in ends to seal tightly. Coat rolls in flour, dip in egg, then roll in breadcrumbs. Place in a flat baking dish and bake, uncovered, in a 350° oven for 20 minutes.

Sauce: Melt remaining butter and herb mixture and stir in wine. Pour over chickens and continue baking, basting occasionally, for about 15 minutes longer or until chicken is brown and tender. Arrange on hot platter, spooning sauce over.

Poulets de Grains ou Suprêmes Véronique
Broilers or Breast of Chicken Veronique
6 servings

6 broilers or 6 chicken breasts
salt, pepper, paprika
¾ cup butter
2 shallots
¼ lb mushrooms
⅓ cup flour
1 tbsp brown sugar
2 to 2½ cups chicken broth, warmed

½ cup white wine
juice of small lemon
rind of small lemon, grated
thyme, bay leaf
2 cups seedless grapes, peeled
a few grape clusters for garnish
½ cup softened butter

Preheat oven to 375°.

Season chicken inside and out with the salt, pepper, and paprika. Melt ½ cup butter in large skillet and brown chicken starting with skin side down. Remove from pan and add ¼ cup butter and sauté the shallots and mushrooms. Cook over medium heat 5 to 6 minutes and then blend in the flour and sugar, adding warmed chicken broth, wine, lemon juice and rind. Bring to a boil and stir. Put chicken into an ovenproof casserole, sprinkle with thyme and add bay leaf. Pour sauce over and braise, covered, in a preheated oven for 30 minutes or until done. Five minutes before serving, add the grapes. Arrange chicken on a hot platter, pour sauce over, and garnish with grape clusters.

Dinde Florentine   Turkey with Spinach and Cream Cheese

10 to 15 lb turkey
2 bunches spinach or
  2 frozen packages
8 oz cream cheese
1 tbsp chives
2 eggs

$\frac{1}{2}$ tsp chopped fresh thyme or
  $\frac{1}{8}$ tsp dry thyme
salt, pepper, nutmeg
3 tbsps butter
turkey giblets, cooked

Clean, wash and boil spinach for 10 minutes, drain, and chop coarsely. Add 2 tbsps butter, salt and pepper and nutmeg, and blend in cream cheese and chives. Add the two eggs and mix well. Stuff the turkey with this mixture, truss cavity and roast it at 350⁰ — 20 minutes to the pound. When browned, cover turkey to keep meat moist. When done cooking, take it out of the pan and make a **roux** with 1 tbsp of butter, 2 tbsps of flour, and add the juice of the turkey or broth.

Chop the giblets previously cooked and add to sauce. Slice turkey and serve, with sauce separate.

Dinde Bordelaise   Bordelaise Turkey

1 turkey 10 to 15 lbs
1 lb cèpes or mushrooms
2 large onions
2 cloves garlic
2 tbsps oil
2 tbsps butter
1 tbsp parsley
3 sprigs chopped thyme or $\frac{1}{8}$ tsp dry

salt and pepper to taste
the turkey liver and the
  cooked giblets
marrow from 2 large bones
1 cup bread crumbs
1 cup seedless grapes
2 eggs
1 bay leaf

Boil the giblets in a court bouillon of water, 1 carrot, 1 medium onion, 2 or 3 leaves of celery, 1 leek if available, salt and pepper, 1 bay leaf, 1 sprig of thyme, 2 or 3 cloves, for 1 hour or until tender enough to chop. Let all come to a boil and simmer. Add *empty* marrow bones and simmer.

Remove mushroom stems. Peel onions and garlic, chop coarsely and sauté in butter or oil; add the chopped stems of mushrooms. Take off heat and add the marrow cut in small pieces, the chopped liver, parsley, chopped giblets, bread crumbs, salt and pepper and thyme, the grapes and eggs. Mix well and stuff the turkey, closing the cavity with thread or skewer, rubbing turkey with goose, chicken or duck fat, or oil. Roast turkey at 350⁰, 20 minutes to the pound, or until tender. When turkey is browned, cover to moisten the meat, and continue roasting until done. Take it out and keep warm.

Skim off fat from pan juices, and add the wine and bouillon and cook (reduce a little if you wish a thicker gravy). Dilute 1 tsp of corn starch in water or broth and cook 1 or 2 minutes more; taste for seasoning. Serve in gravy boat.

Slice turkey and put it on big platter. Sauté several caps of mushrooms very quickly in 2 tbsps of oil, sprinkle with 1 chopped clove of garlic and parsley, salt and pepper, and use to garnish turkey.

Dinde à l'Alsacienne

1 turkey 10 to 15 lbs
6 Strasbourg sausages
2 onions
1½ lbs sauerkraut
1 cup mashed potatoes
thyme (2 or 3 sprigs, or
   ⅛ tsp dry)
1 bay leaf
salt and pepper

Turkey with Sauerkraut Dressing (Good for goose and duck also)

1 egg
½ cup white wine
½ cup broth
1 tsp caraway seed (optional)
½ lb sausage meat or
   fresh ground pork
2 tbsps goose, chicken or
   duck fat, or butter

Slice and sauté the onion in the fat or butter; add sausage meat, 1 cup of sauerkraut, dry mashed potatoes, the optional caraway seed, salt and pepper and the sprigs of thyme chopped, and the egg. Stuff the turkey with the mixture, close cavity with thread or skewers, and roast in a slow oven at 325°, 25 minutes per lb, or until tender. After the turkey has browned, it can be covered to keep meat moist.

Drain the rest of the sauerkraut and cover half-way with boiling water, (if you don't like it too strong, boil it and drain, and add fresh boiling water) and cook simmering for 1 hour. Drain and arrange around the turkey with the 6 Strasbourg sausages, (they are similar to the thin frankfurters of America) and continue roasting. Serve on a large platter surrounded by a bed of sauerkraut, topped with the sliced sausages.

Remove fat from juice of roasting pan, add ½ cup of white wine and ½ cup of broth to the juice, reduce a little and serve with the turkey and sauerkraut. If you want a thicker sauce, add 1 tbsp of corn starch diluted with cold water or juice and simmer a few minutes.

Variation:

Brown Sauce Perigord (with Truffles): In a saucepan, brown together: ⅓ cup flour with ¼ cup sweet butter. Add hot water and ½ cup sherry, (sauce should still be thick, as turkey juice will be added later to thin) and salt and pepper; cook a little longer with a pinch of cloves and allspice — about 20 minutes more. Dice and add truffles; sherry to taste.

Dinde Chipolata

Turkey Chipolata
8 to 10 servings

1 turkey, 8 to 10 lbs. or smaller
1 lb link sausage
1 large onion
1 to 2 tbsps butter
1 lb chestnuts, cooked
½ lb ground veal, chicken
  or turkey
1 slice bread, soaked and drained

1 tbsp aromatic herbs: rosemary, thyme,
  oregano, marjoram, chopped
1 tbsp parsley, chopped
1 egg
1 pinch cloves
1 pinch allspice
salt and pepper

Preheat oven to 375°.

Loosen the skin from the turkey flesh with your hands by sliding them carefully in between so as not to break the skin. Insert the link sausages under the skin.

Sauté the onion in a little butter. Mix the cooked chestnuts with the ground meat, the bread, sautéed onions, herbs and spices. Add the egg and mix well. Fill the turkey with this dressing and close the cavity with skewers or thread. Truss the turkey and tie it.

Bake in preheated oven for 1½ hours, basting the turkey from time to time with butter or drippings. When brown on all sides, cover and reduce heat to 300°. Bake another hour until tender.

Note: Use the neck and gizzard to make broth and use the turkey pan juices and broth to make a giblet gravy.

Dinde aux Olives

Turkey with Green Olives

1 turkey, 10 to 15 lbs
turkey liver and giblets
½ cup dry white wine
½ lb ground veal
1 cup breadcrumbs
¼ lb fresh pork breast

1 can green olives
1 orange
1 cup celery leaves
3 medium onions
2 sprigs fresh thyme or
  ⅛ tsp dried capers

Boil the giblets in water with 1 carrot, 1 onion, and 1 stalk of celery, salt and pepper, until tender, or about 1 hour. Grind the liver and pork together and add to the chopped giblets along with the veal. Sauté the remaining two onions in butter, thyme, salt and pepper, the juice of the orange and 8 chopped green olives, 1 tsp of orange rind grated, capers, parsley. Fill the turkey with stuffing and sew or truss cavity closed. Rub turkey with butter or oil and roast at 350° (20 minutes to the pound), covering turkey with a towel when it is brown until finished cooking (3 to 5 hours).

For sauce, thicken turkey juices with 1 tbsp cornstarch diluted with water or broth or wine, and cook for five minutes more. Slice turkey and pass sauce separately. Garnish with remaining olives (warmed).

Pigeon Casserole Grandmère

Grandmother's Squab Casserole

4 servings

4 pigeons
½ cup butter (part for pigeons,
    part for the onions)
10 small white onions

10 small potatoes Parisienne
½ lb mushrooms
½ lb fresh bacon
salt and pepper

Preheat oven to 350°.

Brown the pigeons in ¼ cup of butter for about 10 minutes, until browned on all sides. Place them in a covered casserole and bake them in the preheated oven for 15 minutes. Peel the onions and sauté them in ¼ cup butter and two tbsps of water. Cover and simmer very slowly for 15 minutes. Peel small potatoes; blanch them for 5 minutes in salted water, then sauté in the butter until golden brown. Peel, wash and sauté the mushrooms with the fresh bacon. After 5 minutes remove the mushrooms, but continue cooking the fresh bacon a little longer. Put all the graniture into the casserole with the pigeons and let cook for 5 minutes more. Serve the pigeons on a heated platter with the garniture around it.

HINT:

To prevent the onions from making you cry, just dip them in boiling water for a few minutes. This will also prevent them from falling apart.

Poussins sur Croutons

Squab on Toast

4 servings

1 squab per serving
salt and pepper
½ lb mushrooms
juice of 1 lemon
1 minced shallot (or white
    part of a green onion)
2 tbsps butter
½ cup sherry

livers from the squabs
2 tbsps butter
1 slice of bread per bird, trimmed
    to fit the birds
2 to 3 oz cognac or brandy
1 egg yolk
⅓ cup heavy cream
1 tsp cornstarch

Season the squabs with salt and pepper, inside and out, and roast in a preheated 375° oven for 25 minutes.

Meanwhile wash the mushrooms and halve or quarter them, depending on their size, and boil them for 5 minutes in lemon juice, water, and a little salt in a stainless steel pan. Strain and reserve some of the liquid.

Continued

Sauté the shallots in butter but do not let them turn brown. Add the mushroom water and sherry and reduce to half. Add the livers and sauté until cooked through, then mash them with a fork. Mix in 2 tbsps butter until smooth. Toast the trimmed bread and spread the liver mixture on it. Set in the oven for a few minutes to warm thoroughly. Warm the cognac or brandy and pour over the squabs; ignite. Place the squabs on the toast slices.

Mix the egg yolk with the cream and stir in the cornstarch. Add to the sauce and stir until it thickens. If the sauce is too thick, thin with broth, sherry or mushroom liquid. Check the seasonings and add nutmeg before spooning over the squabs.

Caneton Montmorency

1 duck, 4 to 5 lbs
2 1-lb cans Bing cherries,
    (dark, pitted cherries),
    drained (reserve the juice)
2 tbsps butter

Duck with Cherries

2 tbsps brandy or port
2 tsp lemon juice
herbs: parsley, thyme, rosemary
salt and pepper
1 slice orange peel

Preheat oven to 400°.

Sauté the drained cherries in butter for 5 minutes. Add the orange peel, brandy, and lemon juice and remove from the heat.

Rub salt and pepper on the duck, inside and out. Place some parsley, thyme and rosemary inside the duck. Put the cherries in the duck and sew up or skewer to close the cavities.

Roast at 400° for 15 minutes; then decrease heat to 375° and continue roasting 1½ hours, or until done. Serve with cherry sauce.

Cherry Sauce:

In the pan in which the cherries were sautéed, mix together the following:

½ cup cherry juice (reserved from the can)

1½ cups chicken stock or duck stock

2 oz brandy

1 tbsp cornstarch, mixed with a little cold water

Bring these ingredients to a boil, stirring until thickened. Add the cherries from the duck after the duck is roasted.

Caneton Franc-Comtois

Duck from Franche-Comté Province

4 to 6 servings

1 duck, 4½ to 5 lbs
2 tbsps butter
2 tbsps oil
½ lb beef (chuck), coarsely chopped
2 large onions, coarsely chopped
2 carrots, coarsely chopped
4 shallots, chopped
1 tbsp flour
½ cup white wine

2 cups brown stock
salt, freshly ground pepper
2 cloves garlic
1 **bouquet garni:** bay leaf, thyme, parsley
½ cup sherry
2 tbsps heavy cream
2 tbsps grated cheese

Preheat oven to 375⁰.

Cut the neck and tips of the wings from the duck. Remove and chop the giblets; reserve the liver. Heat the butter and oil in a heavy pot, add the neck, wing tips, giblets, and coarsely chopped beef. Add the onions, carrots, and shallots. Add the flour and let it brown lightly, then add the white wine, stock, salt, pepper, garlic, and **bouquet garni.** Bring to a boil, lower the heat and simmer for 1½ to 2 hours.

Season the duck with salt and pepper and roast in a 375⁰ oven for 1 hour. Remove the legs and breast and keep them warm. Cut up the carcass. Pour off the fat in the roasting pan and deglaze. Add the carcass and sherry to the sauce pan with the giblets and vegetables, and cook for 10 to 15 minutes longer. Strain the sauce, rubbing the vegetables through a strainer. Bring to a boil again. Cook the liver in a little water until firm; then rub it through the strainer into the sauce. Add the cream and simmer gently for 5 minutes, but do not boil. Keep the sauce warm and adjust seasoning.

Skin the breast of the duck and cut into quarters. Cut the legs at the joint. Make 8 pieces in all. Arrange them on a fireproof serving dish, coat with the sauce, and sprinkle with cheese. Put under the broiler until brown.

Note: The legs can also be served in a separate dish, accompanied by a mixed salad with mustard dressing or a bearnaise sauce.

Canard Nantais aux Olives

Duck with Olives

1½ to 2 cups green olives
1 duck, about 5 lbs
salt, pepper, cayenne pepper
2 tbsps **Parisian Seasoning** (reserve 1 tsp for sauce)

¼ cup butter
3 tbsps flour
¾ cup chicken or duck stock
½ cup red wine
1 clove garlic, minced

Soak olives in water for 24 hours, changing the water three or four times to remove the salt.

Sprinkle the duck cavity generously with salt and sparingly with pepper

Continued

and cayenne. Add a tablespoon of **Parisian Seasoning.** Stuff the duck with the olives.

Rub the outside of the duck generously with salt and cayenne. Tie it securely to a spit, if using a rotisserie, and cook for 1 hour. Or, the duck may be roasted in a 400⁰ oven for an hour (or until crisp on the outside).

Meanwhile, make a **roux** by melting the butter with the flour in the top of a double boiler and cooking until it takes on a brown color. Add the stock, wine, a pinch of cayenne, garlic, salt, and 1 tsp **Parisian Seasoning.** Cook for at least 25 minutes.

To serve: Remove the olives and carve the duck. Each serving should include duck and olives topped with sauce. Serve any remaining sauce separately.

Canard à l'Orange

Duck with Orange
4 servings

1 duck (4 to 5 lbs)
1 piece celery
1 apple, cored
1 orange, peeled and seeded
   (reserve peel)
¼ cup granulated sugar
2 tbsps red wine vinegar
2 cups chicken consomme

1 cup fresh orange juice
2 tbsps currant jelly
½ cup sherry
3 drops tabasco sauce
3 drops orange bitters
salt and pepper
2½ tbsps cornstarch
1 orange, sliced in half rounds
currant jelly, sliced in half rounds

Preheat oven to 325⁰.

Stuff the duck with a piece of celery, apple and peeled orange. Place it breast side up on a rack in a roasting pan. *(Do not add water to the pan.)* Roast at 325⁰ for 1½ to 2 hours, depending on size of duck, until tender.

SAUCE: Peel the orange very thinly, avoiding as much white membrane as possible. Cut the peel in fine julienne strips, place in a sauce pan, cover with boiling water and let stand for a few minutes. Drain and set aside.

Melt the sugar in a saucepan until it carmelizes. Add the wine vinegar, stirring constantly. Add the orange juice, currant jelly, orange rind, and chicken consomme. Cover and simmer for at least ½ hour, then add the sherry, tabasco and orange bitters. Season to taste with salt and pepper.

Combine the cornstarch with a little water and add to the sauce, stirring constantly. Cook until the sauce is thickened and comes to a boil.

Garnish the duck with orange slices and currant jelly cut into half rounds.

Serve the sauce over the duck or separately. Accompany duck with wild rice.

Oie aux Marrons

1 goose, 8 to 10 lbs
1 carrot, peeled
a few celery leaves, chopped
1 onion, studded with cloves
salt and pepper
½ lb cooked ham
1 tbsp herbs (use some of the
    following: tarragon, chervil,
    parsley, thyme, rosemary)

Roasted Goose with Chestnuts

1 onion, for stuffing
½ lb chestnuts, broken
1 small apple per serving
1 jar (10 oz) currant or
    apple jelly
½ lb whole chestnuts
¼ cup butter
1 tbsp cornstarch

Boil the neck and giblets of the goose in just enough water to cover, adding a carrot, a few leaves of celery, a small onion studded with 4 cloves, and salt and pepper. Cook until the giblets are tender, about 1 hour.

Grind together the meat from the neck and giblets, ham, herbs and onion. Add the half pound of broken chestnuts. Fill the goose with this mixture and sew or skewer the openings. Put the goose on a rack in a roasting pan (if desired the goose may be browned under the broiler before being put in the oven to roast.) Roast the goose at 375° for 1½ to 2 hours, basting it with its own juice.

Peel and core the apples, filling the cavity of each with jelly. Place them in the roasting pan to bake about ¾ hour before the goose has finished cooking. Sauté the remaining whole chestnuts in butter and arrange them on the platter with the goose and baked apples. Thicken the juice of the roast with 1 tbsp cornstarch mixed with 2 tbsps cold water. The gravy should not be too thick.

Pheasant Georgette

1 pheasant
¼ lb sweetbreads
juice of three oranges
¼ cup raisins
1 cup white wine
3 tbsps butter or goose fat
3 tbsps oil
3 tbsps **aromatic herbs**

Walnut Sauce:
¼ cup ground walnuts
2 shallots
2 tbsps butter
1 cup broth
¼ cup heavy cream
1 egg yolk
1 tsp paprika

Cut meat into pieces. Flour and fry in fat in skillet. Then add to the skillet the orange juice, wine, salt and pepper, sweetbreads (blanched and fried ahead of time), herbs and raisins. Simmer covered for 45 minutes. Add more wine if necessary.

Serve with Walnut Sauce: Sauté shallots in butter in sauce pan. Add walnuts and broth (chicken is preferable) and continue cooking on low heat for 30 minutes. Deglaze the skillet juices with a little wine and pour over the

Continued

bird; garnish with parsley. Serve sauce over pheasant pieces.

Note: Walnut sauce is also good with pork. It can be served cold, by adding 2 egg yolks and a little cayenne pepper.

Lapin Provencale   Rabbit

4 to 6 servings

For marinade:
  1 onion, chopped
  1 carrot, chopped
  1 cup red wine
  1 to 2 cloves garlic, minced
  ⅛ tsp ground cloves
  several sprigs fresh fennel
  1 bay leaf
  1 sprig thyme (¼ tsp if fried)
  ¼ cup fresh parsley, chopped
1 rabbit, cut up
2 to 4 tbsps oil
salt and pepper

½ cup bouillon
1 tbsp chopped aromatic herbs
  (thyme, bay leaf, sage)
1 tbsp chopped fennel
3 tbsps tomato purée
2 cloves garlic
1 tbsp mustard
2 to 3 **cornichons** chopped
¼ lb pork, made into **lardons**
liver from the rabbit
fresh parsley, chopped (optional)
croutons, for garnish

Mix the marinade together and marinate the rabbit in it for several hours or, preferably, overnight. Turn the rabbit pieces occasionally. When ready to cook remove the rabbit from the marinade and shake off excess moisture, but do not dry. Reserve the marinade.

Preheat oven to 300°.

Heat the oil in a skillet. Dip the rabbit into flour to absorb any moisture, and brown the pieces on all sides in the fat. Place in a baking dish and add salt and pepper. Add the reserved marinade, the bouillon, herbs, tomato purée, garlic and mustard. Bake in a 300° oven for 45 minutes in covered baking dish.

Near the end of the cooking time add the **lardons** and the chopped **cornichons.**

Remove the membrane from the rabbit liver by scraping it with a spoon; chop it into small pieces. When the rabbit has finished cooking, remove the pieces to a heated platter and stir the chopped liver into the pan juices. Pour juices over the rabbit and sprinkle with chopped fresh parsley if desired.

Garnish with croutons.

Le Lapin du Leslée   Rabbit with Herbs and Mushrooms
6 servings

1 young rabbit, cut up (see below)
¼ cup butter or margarine
2 cups dry white wine
1 cup **fond blanc** broth,
  chicken or veal
2 tbsps aromatic herbs: rosemary,
  thyme, fennel

salt and pepper
¼ lb mushrooms
1 shallot, chopped
2 tbsps butter
2 cups cream
parsley, chopped fine,
  for garnish

Cut up the rabbit as follows: cut hind quarters, separting the two legs, cut the back in two pieces, then cut the front part in two or three pieces. Roll pieces in flour.

Heat the butter in a heavy flame-proof casserole and sauté the rabbit on all sides. Add the onions and sauté for a minute or two, then add the wine, the stock and the herbs, except the parsley. Season with salt and pepper, cover and simmer for 1 hour (or the casserole may be put in a 300° oven for 1 hour.)

Take out the rabbit and keep warm. Sauté the mushrooms with the shallot over a fairly high flame; reduce liquid to half. Reduce the heat and add the cream, simmering until slightly thickened. Correct the seasoning and pour the sauce over the rabbit. Sprinkle with parsley to garnish.

BEEF, VEAL, PORK, LAMB

Beef, Veal, Pork, Lamb

I was once decorated by a general. At the time, I was working for the Richard Tobin family in San Francisco. Earlier generations of the Tobins and the Kellys had founded one of our oldest banks, the Hibernia. Following the first World War, Mr. Tobin had been a member of the American delegation to the Paris peace negotiations, and he was later a minister to Holland. So during the Great Conference of 1945* we entertained visitors from all over the world at the house at 1000 Mason Street.

One evening I was called into the dining room at the request of one of the guests, Marine Corps Major General Joseph Smith. As a compliment to my cooking, he took off one of the stars from his uniform and pinned it on me, kissing both of my cheeks in the French accolade. Mrs. Tobin said to me, "Josephine, the general has paid you a very high compliment, and you must always wear his decoration. So I did until the day on the street car when a woman spotted the star and asked if I'd lost a son in the war. I never wore that decoration in public again, though I still have that star and a medal which he gave me on another occasion.

I cooked for many other dignitaries that year, including Admiral Nimitz, Lord Cranborne of Britain, the Ambassador from China and a South African general. My daughter, who collected autographs at the time, got a lot of autographs that year.

---

*United Nations Conference on International Organization which met in San Francisco to draw up the first U.N. charter.

Grillade d'Ampuis

Marinade:
½ cup red wine
1 bay leaf
2 sprigs thyme, chopped
2 sprigs rosemary, chopped
2 sprigs marjoram, chopped
3 tbsps oil
1 onion, chopped
1 carrot, chopped
⅛ tsp pepper

Marinated Broiled Steak
4 to 6 servings

flour, for coating meat
2 lbs rump or skirt steak
2 tbsps oil
2 tbsps butter, melted
a few mushrooms,
    sautéed for garnish
2 tbsps butter
salt and pepper

Combine ingredients to make a marinade and marinate the steak in it for 3 to 4 hours, or preferably overnight.

Remove the meat from the marinade and coat with flour. Brush it with melted butter and oil and put under the broiler for 4 to 5 minutes on each side.

In a saucepan, reduce the marinade to half the original volume, add 2 tbsps butter, salt and pepper. Serve this sauce over the steak and garnish with mushrooms.

Boeuf Isigny Parisienne

1 lb lean beef
1 onion, chopped
butter and oil
1 tbsp flour
2 cups stock, warmed

Beef with Cream
4 servings

1 tsp mustard
salt and pepper
1 pinch nutmeg
½ lb mushrooms, sautéed
½ cup sweet cream

Cut meat into strips, sprinkle with pepper and let stand. To prepare sauce, brown onion in some butter and oil, add flour and then the stock, gradually. Bring to boil, then simmer for 15 to 20 minutes. Add mustard, salt and nutmeg. Sauté meat very quickly in butter and oil. When brown, add to sauce, along with mushrooms; simmer mixture a few minutes, then add sweet cream. When warmed through, serve with rice.

Tournedos Bourguignon

1 large tournedo per serving
1 piece of toasted or fried bread
    per serving (trimmed to
    size of steak)
Bouquet Garni
2 tbsps oil
1 carrot
¼ cup plus 2 tbsps butter

Filet or Top Sirloin Rounds
with Burgundy

2 tbsps finely chopped parsley
1 garlic clove
1 slice bacon or strip
    of fat per serving
salt and pepper
½ cup red wine (Burgundy)
2 limes or lemon
1 carrot, diced

Cut filet or sirloin in neat rounds; combine with oil, red wine, bouquet garni, diced carrot and crushed garlic and marinate for at least 2 hours or overnight. Cut the bread the size of the tournedos. It may be toasted or fried. Dry meat thoroughly. Wrap a piece of bacon or back fat around each. Fry tournedos on one side until brown. (If you wish, they may be fried on both sides for a lesser amount of time.) Place each tournedo fried side down in a shallow broiling pan. Dot each with butter and broil for 5 to 6 minutes (for a rare steak). Discard bacon or back fat; season steak with sale and pepper.

Reduce marinade. Melt ¼ cup butter until a hazelnut color appears. Add the juice of limes or lemons and the marinade. Place meat on bread rounds and pour the sauce over. Sprinkle with parsley.

Boeuf Bourguignon Josephine   Beef Stew Josephine

3 lbs lean stewing beef,
   cut in quite large cubes
2 tbsps oil (Olive)
salt and pepper
2 tbsps flour
1 carrot
1 large onion
1 ½ lbs small white onions

2 cups red wine (hot)
3 cups stock (hot)
1 tbsp tomato paste
2 cloves garlic
thyme
bay leaf
¼ to ½ lb bacon, cut into pieces
¾ to 1 lb mushrooms

Cut beef into large cubes; dry on towels and brown in fat or oil. Brown onion and carrot, season with salt and pepper; add garlic. Arrange meat and vegetables in fireproof casserole, sprinkle flour over it and toss to coat the meat. Let meat brown on top of the stove or in the oven, then stir in hot wine and broth, enough to barely cover meat. Add tomato paste, herbs and bacon; bring to simmer on the stove and then cover and set in lower third of preheated oven (325⁰); simmer for 2 to 2½ hours.

Meanwhile, sauté onions and set aside. Sauté mushrooms in butter for 5 to 6 minutes and set aside. Ten minutes before serving, add onions. When serving, spoon mushrooms on top and sprinkle with parsley.

Chateau Briand a l'Alsacienne   Filet of Beef Wellington

filet of beef (top sirloin or even top round). See note below.
¹/₃ cup sherry, and ¹/₃ cup red wine
1 tsp mustard, dry or prepared (Dijon)
puff pastry, or semi-puff pastry (demi feuilletee) or Brioche Dough (see
   Pastry)
slices of pork fat (barde de lard), suet, or cube of butter
1 each of celery, carrot and onion
½ lb mushrooms
4 to 6 oz foie gras
½ cup ground ham (optional)

Continued

1 cup **fond blanc** (veal or chicken stock)
1 truffle (optional)
1 tbsp tomato purée mixed with a little meat extract or strong bouillon
herbs: fresh ground black pepper, salt, ½ tsp crumbled rosemary, 1 bay leaf,
      chopped parsley, ½ clove garlic crushed.

Note: The filet, of course, is the tenderest cut of all, but very expensive and not the best flavored. The top sirloin and top round have a much better flavor and are not as costly. Buy according to your means and taste. One pound of meat for 3 or 4 persons.

Rub beef with mustard and pepper and pour wine and sherry over (this will tenderize the meat.) Marinate about ½ to 1 hour. Cut all vegetables in small pieces. Spread vegetables, rosemary, bay leaf and parsley over bottom of roasting pan. Take meat out of marinade and tie larding pork or suet over it. Place roast on top of vegetables. Roast 15 mins. to the pound (400⁰) for 25 mins. if the roast is 5 lbs or more; if 2 lbs or under, roast 10 mins. to the pound for very rare. You must roast according to size and desired rareness — *this is very important for a perfect roast.* Remove roast and let cool at room temperature.

Sauté chopped mushrooms and ham in a little butter; add the crushed garlic, pepper and salt. Take garlic out and mix ham and mushrooms with foie gras, truffle and ⅓ cup of the marinade.

Roll out puff pastry in a sheet large enough to wrap the roast. Lay roast on puff pastry. Pile the foie gras mixture on top. Carefully wrap the roast in the pastry, turning in the ends, and press all the seams together. Lay the roast seam side down in a shallow roasting pan. Make a small hole on each end for the steam to escape. Brush pastry with egg mixed with a little milk. Decorate with strips of pastry, rasace or circles, and bake in a hot oven (450⁰) from 25 to 45 mins according to size.

To make sauce, add to the marinade and vegetables in pan, 1 tbsp tomato paste, the broth, and a little tarragon. Heat for 5 to 7 mins. Thicken, if you wish, with 1 tsp cornstarch. Can also be served with a brown sauce, mushroom sauce, or Bearnaise (see *Sauces*).

Note: If your roast is small, it would be advisable to precook the crust (over a loaf mold) as the crust will take longer to cook than the meat. Then put meat inside and top it with another piece of crust and decorate as above.

Boeuf à la Mode — en Gelée   **Beef in Aspic**

4 or 5 lbs coulotte
   or eye round of beef
½ lb salted pork, cut
   in strips
salt and pepper (ground)
½ tsp mace

½ cup brandy
2 or 3 tbsps beef fat,
   bacon fat or oil
2 calf's feet (if not available
   use pig's feet) cut in
   4 pieces

Sauce:

3 cups dry white wine
1 large onion
2 carrots
2 shallots or white of
    green onion, chopped
additional 1 or 2 cups beef consommé

thyme
2 bay leaves
2 sticks celery chopped or sliced
2 or 3 cloves garlic
parsley

The vegetables:

15 small onions   6 carrots (whole)   6 to 8 green beans

Lard meat or have it done by butcher. To do this, make incision in beef and push salt pork into it. (Be sure to leave salt pork in water awhile to unsalt it a little.) Be careful not to put too much salt pork in the pot roast. Sprinkle meat with salt, pepper and mace. Place meat in bowl, pour brandy over it, and marinate 3 to 4 hours, turning meat occasionally. Remove beef (reserving marinade), wipe dry, and brown on all sides in hot fat or oil. Transfer meat to cooking pot and keep warm. Wipe calf's or pig's feet dry and brown in same saucepan as used for browning beef. DO NOT SCRAPE THE PAN or the jelly will be cloudy. Deglaze pan with a little consommé and save for another purpose.

If you wish a sauce: add wine and marinade to meat. Peel and add onion, 2 carrots, celery, bay leaf, parsley and cloves. Let all come to boil and simmer 4 hours. Let cool. Skim off and discard all fat. Strain juice in fine strainer. Add juice to 2 more cups of consommé and simmer slowly 15 minutes or more to clarify.

Jelly: To 2 cups of consommé add 1 tbsp gelatin dissolved in a little cold water. (If you do not use the feet in the pot roast, add a little more gelatin.) Pour enough of the jelly to coat the bottom of the mold. Chill until set.

The vegetables: Cook the vegetables in water until tender. Cut 2 inches from small ends of carrots. Split and arrange them daisy fashion in mold. Finish covering the bottom with the rest of carrots. Slice the onions and beans in two. Bend to form a circle around onions with semi-liquid stock. Chill until firm.

Finish filling the mold with slices of beef and meat from feet cut into *julienne.* Pour in enough of reserved stock to cover the meat. Chill until ready. Unmold on platter and garnish with parsley.

Foie de Genisse Roti

Roasted Baby Beef Liver
4 to 6 servings

1 lb liver (whole)
1 cup milk
¼ lb mushrooms
2 fatback strips
1 lemon
1 bay leaf
⅓ cup cream
2 tbsps oil
4 tbsps butter

¼ lb fresh breast of pork,
    cooked for ¾ hour
1 large onion
1 stalk celery leaves
a sprig of thyme
1 tbsp flour
salt and pepper
1 cup broth

Continued

Preheat oven to 375⁰.

Cover liver with milk for ½ day or overnight. One hour before cooking, take it out and dry (put some flour on a board to set liver on, then put some more flour on the other side of liver. This method is better than using a paper towel as it keeps the juices in the meat.) Keep milk for use later. Cut a few narrow strips of pre-cooked pork and insert in liver with a larding needle or pointed knife.

In a frying pan put 2 tbsps oil and sauté liver on both sides very quickly to brown slightly; then lay it on a piece of fatback, with salt and pepper, bay leaf and thyme, and lay another strip of fatback on top and tie it.

Cut the remaining breast of pork into dices, adding the chopped onion, celery, mushrooms and rind of one lemon and sauté together. Cook for a while, then put it in bottom of fireproof dish, with the liver placed on top.

In a frying pan melt 2 tbsps butter. Add the milk from the liver marinade and then add ¹/₃ cup of cream. Let it come to a boil and pour over the liver, and set in a preheated oven for 15 minutes.

In the meantime, melt the 2 remaining tbsps of butter, add a tbsp flour, stir, and add the warm broth, salt and pepper. After 15 minutes, take liver out, pour this sauce over, and bake again another 15 minutes. The liver will be pink when sliced. Put vegetables around and serve hot.

Langue de Boeuf Aigre - Douce   Sweet and Sour Beef Tongue

1 beef tongue (fresh)	1 carrot
1 onion	1 stalk of celery
1 leek	2 or 3 cloves
thyme	laurel (bay leaf)
salt and pepper	water

Rub tongue with salt 24 hours before cooking. Place tongue in a soup kettle, large enough to hold it comfortably. Cover over with water by 1 to 2 inches, bring it to a boil, skim off scum and reduce heat to simmer. Add the vegetables, spices and herbs. Simmer for about 2 hours, covered, leaving a little opening for air. Remove tongue and trim and skin. Remove small bones and fat. Tongue is then braised for 1 hour more or until tender.

To braise, use the following ingredients:

2 tbsps butter	2 tbsps oil
1 diced carrot	salt and pepper
onion	1 cup beef broth (from tongue)
celery	1 glass vinegar
1 glass white wine	1 tsp mustard
1 tbsp tomato paste	2 tbsps flour
thyme	½ cup currants or
bay leaves	Smyrna raisins (soaked in a
2 tbsps currant jelly	little water)
3 cloves	

In butter and oil brown the tongue on all sides. Take out. In same fat, put in flour, adding more butter if necessary, and stir until brown. Add carrot, onion, celery, wine, broth, tomato paste, thyme, bay leaf and stud with cloves. Put tongue back in and bring it to a boil, simmering on top of stove or in 300⁰ oven for 1 hour or until tender.

Mix jelly, vinegar, mustard and add to tongue; then add the raisins, and continue simmering until tongue is tender. To serve, slice and pour sauce over. If sauce is too thin for your taste, dilute 1 tsp cornstarch in a little wine and add to sauce. Sprinkle with parsley.

Langue de Boeuf Turinoise · Beef Tongue, Turin

¼ lb fresh or smoked bacon
½ cup white wine
½ cup juice from tongue
rind of one orange
½ cup ginger
breadcrumbs or ginger wafers
salt

a mirepoix of onion, carrot,
celery, thyme, bay leaf
2 tbsps vinegar
rind of one lemon
2 tbsps oil
2 tbsps butter
pepper

Boil and braise as in Langue de Boeuf Aigre Douce recipe. Blanch bacon 10 minutes in water and dice. Brown in oil and butter. Add tongue, wine, broth, vegetable, salt and pepper.

Boil orange and lemon rind in water for 5 minutes and add to tongue. Simmer on top of stove or in a 300⁰ oven for one hour until tender.

Fifteen minutes before cooking ends, soak ginger bread crumbs in vinegar, slice and pour sauce over.

Cotelettes de Veau Provençale · Veal Chops Provençal

6 servings

3 to 4 onions, sliced
butter
1 tsp flour
1 cup white wine
6 veal chops

½ cup broth
salt and pepper
flour
1 small can black olives

Sauté onions in butter until transparent. Stir in flour and half the wine. Season with salt and pepper and set aside. Lightly flour the veal chops and sauté in butter until golden brown. Add remaining wine along with broth and simmer for 45 minutes. Add a few black olives, then transfer with chops to a platter and surround with the onions. Can be served with grilled tomatoes.

Poitrine de Veau Farcie

Stuffed Breast of
Veal, Boiled or Roasted
6 to 8 servings

½ lb spinach, cooked, chopped
  and squeezed dry
3 slices bread
¾ cup milk
1 onion, finely chopped
3 cloves garlic, minced
4 tbsps butter
¼ lb sweetbreads
¼ lb pork, ground
¼ lb veal, ground
¼ lb pork fat
⅓ cup Gruyère or other
  Swiss-type cheese

1 tsp parsley
1 tsp sage
¼ tsp marjoram
¼ tsp thyme
⅛ tsp cloves
1 tbsp salt
1 tsp pepper
2 hard-cooked eggs, chopped
  (optional)
½ cup pistachio nuts
4 to 5 lbs breast of veal, with pocket
vegetables (see below) if veal
  is to be boiled

Stuffing: Prepare the spinach and soak the bread in milk. Sauté the onions and garlic in 2 tbsps butter. Sauté the sweetbreads in 2 tbsps butter and transfer, with the onions and garlic, to a mixing bowl. Add the pork, veal, pork fat, cheese, spinach, herbs and spices. Add the chopped, hard-cooked eggs, if desired, and mix all together. Squeeze excess milk from the bread. Add the bread, mix with the other ingredients and fold in the pistachio nuts.

Fill the veal pocket with the stuffing and sew up the opening of the pocket with thread or close it with skewers. Veal may be roasted or boiled.

To roast the veal: Brown the stuffed breast of veal on all sides and bake it in a covered roasting pan, set on the center rack of the oven. Bake for 1½ hours at 350⁰ to 375⁰. Serve hot or cold.

To boil the veal: Place onion halves, garlic clove, a chopped carrot, a bay leaf and parsley in a large roaster or soup kettle and lay the stuffed veal on top. Add enough broth or water to barely cover the meat. Salt and pepper to taste. Bring to a boil, reduce the heat, cover and simmer for 1¼ hours.

Serve hot or cold.

Escalopes de Veau à l'Alsatienne

Alsatian Scallopini

2 very thin scallops
  of veal per serving
  (butcher will prepare for you)
¼ lb chopped ham
¼ lb chicken or goose livers
1 onion, chopped fine
1 clove garlic, minced
1 tbsp parsley, chopped fine

6 juniper berries, crushed fine
1 truffle (optional)
4 tbsps butter
6 tbsps oil
8 oz Riesling wine
salt and pepper
⅛ tsp thyme
bay leaf
¼ lb mushrooms, sliced

Dry veal scallops and salt and pepper them lightly. Set aside. Chop livers into small pieces. Mix the livers, ham, onions, crushed berries, and truffles (black chopped olives could be used instead for color), and sauté in 2 tbsps butter and 2 tbsps of the oil.

Now spread scallops with ham and liver mixture. Roll and secure with a toothpick or kitchen thread. Roll in flour and sauté in 2 tbsps butter, 2 tbsps oil until golden brown. Arrange in an ovenproof casserole and add wine, thyme, and bay leaf. Bake in a 375^0 oven for 20 to 25 minutes.

Meanwhile, sauté mushrooms in a little oil for 5 or 6 minutes before adding garlic, parsley, salt, and pepper. Sauté for a few minutes more, or until done.

To Serve: Arrange scallops on hot platter and pour mushrooms around. Reduce juices from cooking the scallops to one cup and pour over all or serve separately.

Paupiettes de Veau à la Jardiniere

Rolled Veal Scallops with Vegetables

The paupiettes are made of veal (from the rump or round) cut in slices rather thin and rolled up after having been spread with forcemeat or any other ingredients.

12 scallops	¼ cup butter
½ lb ground veal	2 tbsps oil
½ cup white wine, sauterne or chablis	2 egg yolks
¼ lb mushrooms	pork rind already cooked
2 slices bread, crumpled up	bouquet garni of thyme,
¼ cup bouillon	laurel, rosemary

Mix ground veal, the mushrooms, the bread, and the egg yolks to a fine paste, put through blender or a fine sieve, and add salt and pepper. Smear one side of each scallop with this mixture, roll and fasten with string or tooth pick.

Sauté veal rolls in butter and oil on all sides. Lay pork rind in the bottom of a fireproof casserole, and add veal rolls, wine, bouillon and one bouquet garni of thyme, laurel and rosemary.

Braise in a preheated oven at 300^0 for one hour.

Remove veal to a platter; reduce juice and pour over veal.

Serve with *croustades,* filled with peas cooked in butter with shredded lettuce and onions, string beans cut in small pieces, and small dices of ham (optional).

Cotelettes de Veau Dauphinoise

Veal Chops with Cheese Sauce

6 veal chops
1/3 cup cream
1 cup white wine
1 cup veal or chicken broth
1/4 cup butter
juice of 1 lemon
1 shallot
salt and pepper
1/2 lb mushrooms, sautéed

Cheese Sauce:
1/2 cup ham, sautéed
3/4 cup flour
3/4 cup melted butter
salt and pepper
nutmeg
2 cups milk
3/4 cup cheese
4 egg yolks, beaten

Salt and pepper the chops and sauté in butter over a slow fire, for about 12 to 15 minutes on each side. Deglaze the pan with wine and add a small amount of butter. Keep meat warm.

Prepare cheese sauce. Melt butter in double boiler, adding flour and milk that has been warmed. Add salt, pepper and nutmeg and cook 25 minutes. Add the cheese, yolks and ham (cut into fine strips). Cook for 4 to 5 minutes more.

To serve, transfer meat to a fireproof dish. Cover with the cheese sauce and place under the broiler until browned. Place chops on a platter and pour de-glazed juices over them. Garnish with sautéed mushrooms and shallot, mixed with lemon and cream.

Rignon de Veau Flambés

Flamed Veal Kidneys
4 servings

2 or 3 veal kidneys
1/4 cup butter
1/4 lb fresh or smoked bacon

1/4 cup cognac or brandy
salt and pepper
parsley

Strip off all fat from the kidneys. Warm butter in a frying pan and sauté kidneys very quickly for 5 minutes. Remove kidneys and sauté the diced bacon; cook slowly a few minutes. When they are cooked, return the kidneys to the pan and cook very slowly for 10 to 15 minutes more. Warm the cognac or brandy, pour over the kidneys and ignite, and season with salt and pepper. Set the meat on a warm platter and sprinkle with parsley. Serve with french fried or mashed potatoes.

Cotes de Porc, Sauce Charcutiere

Pork Chops Charcutiere

1 or 2 pork chops per serving
1 liquor glass brandy or cognac
2 or 3 shallots, or whites
   of green onions
1/2 cup wine vinegar,
   white or red

1 cup white wine per serving
1 cup *demi-glace sauce*
3 French cornichons (small
   sour pickles)
chopped parsley

Trim chops of excess fat, and make incisions with a sharp knife on the edges to prevent curling. Fry in fairly hot fat for about 10 minutes on each side. Pork should be well-cooked but not overdone. Ignite with brandy, and take chops from the pan and keep warm.

Charcutiere Sauce: In same fat, sauté shallots; deglaze pan with ½ cup vinegar and the white wine. Transfer to a small pan or double boiler and reduce to ½ cup; add cornichons and 1 cup of demi-glace sauce. Arrange pork chops on a serving platter, coat each with sauce, and serve remaining sauce in gravy boat. Sprinkle with parsley.

Côtes de Porc aux Epices

Pork Steaks with Allspice

pork steaks (tenderloin or chops)
  1 per serving
flour
chicken fat or any other fat
  for browning
salt and pepper

Marinade:
½ to 1 tsp allspice or ⅛ tsp each
  cinnamon, cloves (ground), nutmeg,
  pepper
bay leaf
spring thyme
oregano
rosemary
sage
white wine, Marsala or Port

Marinate pork steaks overnight in marinade. When ready to prepare, dry thoroughly and flour. Brown in a heavy-bottomed skillet that has a tight-fitting lid. Season with salt and pepper and add marinade, adding more wine if necessary. Bring to a boil on top of the stove, cover, and bake in a pre-heated 350° oven for 30 to 45 minutes, making sure not to overcook. Remove steaks to heated platter and spoon pan juices over. If necessary, add more wine to juices first.

Roti de Porc, Sauce Soubise

Roast Pork with Sauce Soubise
8 servings

3½ to 4 lb pork butt roast,
  boned
herbs for stuffing: several sprigs
  of fresh chervil, parsley, thyme,
  rosemary, fennel
2 or 3 cloves garlic, minced
salt and pepper
pork fat

2 carrots, sliced
2 bay leaves
sprig thyme
¼ cup sliced celery leaves
1½ to 2 cups sherry
chopped parsley
Sauce Soubise (see *Sauces*)

Stuff boned section of roast with fresh herbs and garlic. Season with salt

Continued

and pepper. Place more sprigs on top of roast and tie. Sear roast on all sides in the pork fat. Place in roasting pan along with the carrots, bay leaves, thyme, celery, salt and pepper. Add the sherry and cover. Cook in a preheated 250⁰ oven for 1¾ to 2 hours or until done.

To serve: slice the roast and place on a heated platter. Dab each slice with the sauce and sprinkle with chopped parsley. Serve any remaining sauce on the side.

Gigot Romarin

Lamb with Rosemary
5 to 6 servings

1 4 to 5 lbs leg of lamb
mustard to coat lamb
   (Dijon preferred)
fresh rosemary
1 or 2 tbsps oil

4 to 6 cloves garlic
1 recipe Sauce Bordelaise
   (see *Sauces*)
salt and pepper

Preheat oven to 375⁰.

Heat oil and sear lamb on all sides — in a large skillet. Remove from heat and make a few slits on each side of lamb. Insert garlic cloves. Smear the mustard on the lamb and press on the rosemary. Place lamb in a roasting pan and roast at 375⁰ for 30 minutes. Season with salt and pepper, cover, and continue roasting to desired doneness. The meat will be pink near the bone in about 1¼ hours. When ready to serve, scrape the rosemary off the meat. Slice the meat and place on a heated platter. Strain the pan juices into the heated Sauce Bordelaise and pour the sauce over the meat. Serve any remaining sauce on the side.

Poitrine d'Agneau ou Mouton Braisée Florentine
Stuffed Breast of Lamb Florentine
6 to 8 servings

4 lbs boned breast of lamb
2 lbs fresh spinach or
   1½ packages frozen spinach
6 tbsps butter or margarine
2 diced fresh tomatoes, sautéed,
   or 1 cup well drained
   canned tomatoes
6 cups Potatoes Dauphine
   (see *Vegetables*)
⅛ tsp nutmeg

1 onion
1 carrot, sliced
thyme
rosemary
bay leaf
salt, coarse ground black pepper
dash of sugar
1 cup lamb, veal or
   chicken broth
1 cup demi-glace sauce (see *Sauces*)

Flatten the breast of lamb with a mallet or cleaver, and sprinkle with salt and pepper. Set aside. Cook the spinach and drain, seasoning with salt, pepper, nutmeg, butter and sugar. Spread spinach and sautéed tomatoes over the breast of lamb. (Save some spinach as garnish.) Roll the breast and tie with string. Brown lamb on all sides, either in a Dutch oven or roasting pan at 450°; when browned, reduce to 325°-350°, and add broth, sliced carrots, onion and herbs. Cook for about 1½ hours (if broth boils during this time, reduce heat to 300°, and add more broth as needed). Arrange the lamb on a warm platter, garnish with remaining spinach, and surround with Potatoes Dauphine. For sauce, strain the pan juices and bring to a boil; add demi-glace sauce or a bouillon cube dissolved in ½ cup broth, and 1 tsp cornstarch. Serve either over lamb or in a gravy boat.

Epigrammes St. Germain

Breast of Lamb with Peas

4 servings

1 breast of lamb
4 lamb chops (optional)
1 cup white wine
1 carrot
1 stalk celery
1 onion
1 bay leaf
1 sprig thyme

4 cloves
4 parsley stems
salt and pepper to taste
2 egg whites or one whole
  egg, beaten
breadcrumbs
fat for frying (chicken or
  bacon)
2 lbs fresh peas, or ½ lb
  dry split peas

Braise breast of lamb with wine, carrot, celery and onion, with herbs and spices, for ¾ of an hour to 1 hour. Keep the braising liquid below the simmering point.

Place cooked breast of lamb beneath a weight to flatten it as it cools; remove bones and cartilage as well as membranes and fat (ask butcher not to make any cuts in the breast as it will fall apart when you bone it).

Prepare a breading (pane a l'anglaise) as follows: Cut heart shaped pieces of the breast of lamb and roll them first in flour, then in beaten egg whites, and finally in breadcrumbs. Fry the pieces in soft fat such as chicken or bacon fat (not in hard fat such as beef or veal). Season lamb with salt and pepper.

Boil peas rapidly until done and force them through the large holes of a collander to make a purée. Leave out skins of the peas that remain in the collander. Season the purée with butter, salt and pepper.

Arrange the lamb on a platter around a mound of peas and alternate them with broiled lamb chops. Serve with a light curry sauce (see *Sauces*) or the juice of the lamb slightly thickened with cornstarch or **beurre manie** (see *Sauces*).

Gigot au Gingembre

Leg of Lamb with Ginger

leg of lamb
2 inch piece of ginger root
3 or 4 cloves of garlic, slivered
rosemary
powdered ginger
salt and pepper
2 tbsps butter
1 tbsp oil

Sauce:
2 tbsps clarified buerre
   noisette (browned butter)
2 tbsps flour
1 cup *fond brun* (brown stock)
¼ to ½ cup finely chopped
   ginger root
1 tbsp tomato paste
salt and pepper

Season lamb with salt and powdered ginger, preferably the night before. When ready to cook, sear meat on all sides in the butter and oil. Then make deep slits in meat and put in slices of ginger root, slivered garlic and rosemary. Pepper meat.

Place lamb in a roasting pan and cook in a preheated 375⁰ oven. An average-size leg of lamb will need no more than 1¼ hours for meat to be pink at the bone. Cover meat the last 30 minutes of cooking.

Sauce: Sauté ginger in the buerre noisette. Stir in flour and cook until brown in color. Stir in 1 cup of warm *fond brun* and the tomato paste. Add salt and pepper to taste.

Gigot Martiniquaise — Sauce Coloniale
Lamb with Coffee and Sauce Coloniale

6 to 8 servings

1 leg of lamb, 4 to 5 lbs
½ cup mustard (Dijon preferred),
   more if necessary
4 or 5 cloves garlic
several sprigs fresh rosemary
½ to 1 cup strong coffee (can be
   made with 2 tbsps instant)
½ to 1 cup heavy cream
salt and pepper
oil to brown lamb
chopped parsley
1 tbsp shredded coconut
   (optional)

Sauce:
4 tbsps butter
¹/₃ cup flour
1 or 2 shallots, chopped fine
   or 1 small onion

½ cup fine chopped pineapple,
   gooseberry, or mango
1 tbsp curry powder
1 tbsp fine chopped ginger
1 lemon, juice and rind or
   1 cup white wine
1 tbsp tomato concentrate
   or ketchup
1 tbsp Worcestershire
pinch allspice
1 tsp green peppercorns
   (more if desired)
tarragon, chervil, parsley,
   thyme, oregano
1 tbsp current jelly (or sugar)
1 cup stock: beef, chicken, or
   lamb (warmed)

Brown lamb completely in the hot oil to sear all sides. Remove, make slits, and fill slits with garlic cloves and sprigs of rosemary. Season with salt and pepper and coat lamb with the mustard. Place in a roasting pan and cook in a 375⁰ oven for 1 hour. Meat will be pink in the center — adjust cooking time for personal preference. Prepare coffee baste by boiling the cream with the strong coffee. After lamb has cooked for 20 minutes, baste with half of this mixture. Paste again with the rest of this mixture after another 20 minutes.

Meanwhile, prepare sauce by melting butter in a heavy-bottom saucepan. Add shallots and sauté for a minute. Add the flour and cook until flour takes on a brown color. Add the curry powder and cook for another minute. Slowly add the warmed stock and stir until mixture is smooth. Stir in the pineapple, ginger, allspice, lemon, tomato, Worcestershire, peppercorns, and salt. Cover and cook 20 to 25 minutes. When lamb has finished cooking, remove from the oven and drain oven juices into the sauce, being careful not to thin the sauce too much. Add the herbs and jelly to the sauce.

To Serve: Slice lamb and spoon sauce over. Sprinkle with the shredded coconut and/or chopped parsley.

Langues de Mouton Braisées Sauce Blanche au Capres
Lamb Tongues with Caper Sauce

1 ½ lbs lamb tongues
Court Bouillon:
6 cups chicken stock
1 carrot
1 celery stalk
½ tsp thyme
1 bay leaf
1 onion
parsley stems
Sauce:
⅓ cup flour
½ cube butter
⅛ tsp nutmeg

Mirepoix:
oil
butter
½ small onion, coarsely chopped
½ cup chopped celery leaves
1 sliced carrot
1 bay leaf
½ tsp thyme

salt and pepper
2 tbsps drained capers
¼ cup cream
finely chopped parsley

Simmer lamb tongues in court bouillon for two hours or until tender. Peel tongues. Sauté *mirepoix* in olive oil and butter mixture. Remove mirepoix to a casserole with a tight fitting lid. Brown tongues well and add to casserole. Pour 1 cup of tongue broth over tongues, add bay leaf, salt, pepper and thyme. Cover and set in preheated 375⁰ oven for 25 minutes.

For Sauce: make a roux using flour and butter. Stir in two cups lamb broth slowly, stopping when sauce is consistency desired. Add nutmeg and capers. Before serving, add the cream to the sauce.

Remove tongues from casserole and place on a serving dish. Cover with sauce. Sprinkle with chopped parsley.

Ris de Veau Isigny Josephine

1 lb sweetbreads
  (for 3 servings)
¼ lb fresh mushrooms (they must
  be very white and small)
¼ cup butter or margarine,
  clarified (or 2 tbsps oil)
2 shallots or
  white of scallions
juice of 1 lemon

Sweetbread Isigny Josephine

½ cup *cremé frâiche*
  (or heavy cream)
salt and pepper
1 oz cognac or brandy
1 or 2 egg yolks
parsley or chervil or
  tarragon
fried triangles of bread

Sauté the sweetbreads until lightly golden brown; add the chopped shallots or scallions. Add cognac and ignite, and when extinguished, add ⅓ cup of the cooking juice and simmer for 10 to 15 minutes. Sauté the mushrooms in butter just to coat them without browning. (If they are too big, cut into quarters, and if the skin is brown, they must be peeled). Add to sweetbreads and simmer for 5 minutes more (a few drops of blanching water from the sweetbreads and lemon juice may be added if too dry). Mix yolks with cream and add to the sweetbreads and remove from heat. Place on a warm serving dish, sprinkle with parsley, and arrange triangles of bread around meat, or serve in patty shells.

 ## HINT: Cervelle (Brains)

Before being put to use, brains must first be freed of any blood attached to them by soaking and taking off the little pellicule (skin) around them. They should be cooked in a *court bouillon.*

The recipes for and preparation of brains can be applied to any kind of brains, but calf brains are usually considered the best.

One pound of brains will serve about four (4) people. Soak the brains in cold water for one hour. Simmer (do not boil) in *court bouillon* for 15 minutes, drain and remove the skin, blood and cartilage. Then follow any recipe for final preparation.

Cervelle Provençale

Brains Provençale
4 to 6 servings

6 lamb brains
salt and pepper
flour
breadcrumbs
¼ cup butter

1 cup tomato fondue (see *Sauces*)
1 cup black olives
1 tsp tarragon
1 tbsp oil

Cut the brains in slices and season with salt and pepper. Roll the slices in flour, then in breadcrumbs, and fry lightly in oil and butter.

Set the tomato fondue in the center of a platter. Arrange the brains around it. Garnish with olives and sprinkle with chopped tarragon.

Cervelle au Gratin

Gratin of Brains
4 servings

2 brains
breadcrumbs
½ juice of lemon
grated cheese
1 clove garlic

½ lb mushrooms
¼ cup butter
chopped parsley
flour

Slice brains cooked in *court bouillon* and cool. Roll in flour and fry lightly. Arrange in a fireproof dish and coat with a Duxelle sauce (see below). Put on each slice a cooked mushroom. Cover with Duxelle sauce, sprinkle with breadcrumbs mixed with the cheese and brown under the broiler a few seconds. Chop the stems and caps of the mushrooms, reserving enough for each slice of brains. Sauté in butter, add parsley and garlic and spread over slices of brains.

Duxelle Sauce

Sauce Duxelle

Chop 5 or 6 mushrooms, stems and caps and sauté in butter. Add a chopped shallot, 1 clove of garlic, chopped parsley, 2 tbsps of flour and one cup of white wine; cook down. Stir in 1 tbsp of sauce demiglace and 1 tbsp of tomato paste. At the last minute add a small piece of butter and 1 tsp parsley.

Mousse Brestoise

4 to 6 servings

1 lb chicken livers, poached
  briefly, until firm but
  slightly pink
½ lb sweetbreads (peel when fresh)
2 shallots
1 tbsp parsley
1 tsp aromatic herbs (sage,
  rosemary, oregano, thyme,
  marjoram)

¼ lb bacon (4 slices)
1 slice bread, soaked in
  broth or cream
5 to 6 tbsps cream
1 tsp nutmeg
1 tsp allspice
2 egg whites
1 tsp salt
¼ tsp pepper

Preheat oven to 350°.
Purée all ingredients except egg whites in blender (do a little at a time) or in a food processor.
Beat the egg whites with a pinch of salt and mix into the puréed mixture. Turn the mixture into a large buttered mold or individual molds.
Bake at 350° for 15 to 20 minutes.
Unmold and serve with tomato sauce (see *Sauces*).

PASTRY DOUGH, BREAD AND CREPES

Pastry Dough, Bread and Crêpes

I met Charles in 1925 while I worked at the Fleishhackers. They had a manager for their 85-acre estate who used the land to raise cows and chickens. Mrs. Fleishhacker often gave me eggs and cheese and butter to take to her friend Mme. Cotain who lived on Fillmore Street. Every week I would go to her house and one week, one of her boarders was there. He was a good-looking boy, but so sad! He looked so sad that I asked Mme. Cotain, "What is wrong with that boy?" She said, "If you had had his youth, you would be sad, too. He didn't have a happy youth." I made up my mind to marry him and invited him to dinner at Mme. Cotain's house. Charles came, that's who he was, and he brought Louis, his Vaudeville partner.

At the time, Charles played the accordion for the Orpheum Theatre on the Vaudeville circuit. He used to travel from little town to little town, but he never could save any money. When I asked him to marry me, he said that he couldn't ~ he had no money. I told him that was alright ~ after all, I had a good job. Then he said that he owed money to his uncle too. I told him that was alright, too. I'd pay the debt to his uncle. Two weeks later we were married. We moved into a one-room apartment at Washington and Fillmore. It was difficult for both of us then, but we were young and active and worked very hard. We have always been very happy together. We were so poor there that our idea of an evening out was to go watch the neon signs (which had just been introduced) and the lights at Civic Center.

When talking pictures came in, there was no more Vaudeville, and Charles had to change jobs. He began working for Yellow Cab Company, driving for them for the next thirty-one years. But he is still a marvelous accordion player.

We have one daughter, Jacqueline, and she has given us four wonderful grandsons.

Pâte Brisée Fine   Pastry for Pies, Pâtes, Quiches

1 cup flour
½ tsp salt
½ tsp sugar (if to be used
   for a sweet filling)

6 tbsps butter or margarine, cold
1 egg yolk (see *Note*)
a little water (ice water
   if available), about 2 to 3 tbsps

Place the dry ingredients in a mixing bowl and rub in the cold butter with the fingers until the mixture becomes granulated, like cornmeal. Beat the egg yolk with 2 to 3 tbsps of water to make about ¼ cup liquid. Add the liquid to the flour-butter mixture and blend quickly, until the dough can be pressed into a firm ball. It must not be sticky.

Place the dough on a floured board and **fraise** it. (**Fraisage** means to press the pastry with the heel of the hand, not the palm. Press away from you in a quick firm touch of the heel of the hand.) Form quickly into a round ball, sprinkle lightly with flour and wrap in waxed paper or a cloth. Place in the refrigerator for at least two hours or overnight. This pastry will keep one day in the refrigerator or a month or more if frozen. If kept any longer than a day, it is best to freeze it. When ready to use, roll out to desired thickness on a lightly floured board.

To precook pie shell; roll out and put into the pie pan. Press well against the edges. Put foil over the crust, pushing it down well against the dough. Weight it with beans and bake at 375⁰ for 15 minutes. Remove the foil and return the crust to the oven for 10 minutes or as long as necessary to brown it slightly.

Note: Do not use the egg yolk if the crust is to be used for a filling which contains eggs. Without the eggs it is called **Pâte Brisée.**

Pâte à Brioche   Brioche Dough

"Ten pages in the cookbook for the average American brioche — for mine, one-half page."

Ingredients for sponge:
1 envelope dry yeast
½ cup lukewarm water or milk
⅓ cup flour

1 tsp sugar
1 pinch salt (⅛ tsp)

Dissolve the yeast with the water or milk, add pinch of salt and the sugar. Mix in the flour to form a soft ball. Put in a buttered bowl and let sponge rise until it doubles in size.

Method for Brioches:
3⅔ cups flour
½ lb butter or margarine melted
⅓ cup sugar

4 or 5 eggs
raised sponge

Work the butter with flour, add sugar and salt, and the eggs one at a time to make a very soft dough, but not liquid. Knead until it becomes a very smooth paste (almost elastic). Add the raised sponge, mix well, and put in the buttered bowl.

Let stand for 2 to 2½ hours (at 70° to 75°) until double in bulk. Punch down, cover with a plastic bag and put in refrigerator for 2½ hours at least, or overnight. *For best results, keep overnight.* Afterward, grease some fluted molds, or one large one, fill ²/₃ full, make a cross with a knife and insert small ball of the dough to make the head, and let it rise again. Bake at 400°, 15 to 20 minutes for small ones; 30 to 35 minutes for larger ones.

Pâte Feuilletée   Puff Pastry, for Turnovers, Patty Shells, Dessert Pastries and Cookies

4 cups flour (sift before measuring)
1½ cups water, more as needed
1 lb butter or margarine at room temperature
⅛ tsp salt if using unsalted butter or margerine

Put flour in a bowl and add enough water to make a dough soft enough to roll. Knead dough until it is smooth and elastic, 10 to 15 minutes. Slam down on board three times and let rest, covered, in refirgerator 10 minutes. Mold butter into one large cube. Roll the dough into a circle on a well-floured board and place the butter in the center. Fold over four flaps of dough to completely envelop the butter. Turn dough over and roll again, first in one direction and then another in order to form a large one inch thick square. Butter might leak through while rolling, but it will eventually be incorporated correctly.

Do not turn dough over while rolling it out. It will be necessary to flour the board often to keep the dough from sticking. After forming the square, fold into thirds by folding first the left flap and then the right flap on top of that. Roll dough again and fold into thirds. This operation is termed a "turn." The dough will now have two "turns." Dent with two finger marks to mark the turns, and place in plastic bag and refrigerate an hour or more to chill dough completely. This prevents it from becoming too elastic and difficult to work with.

Remove it from the refrigerator and give two more turns. Dent with four marks and refrigerate until ready to use. This paste is better when made a day or more before you intend to use it. It will keep ten days in the refrigerator and up to six months in the freezer. When ready to use, give the dough two final turns.

Roll out dough and shape accordingly. Seal edges with water and prick top for turnovers. In general, the baking temperature is 400° for 10 minutes, 300° for 30 minutes. Remember this is in general: if necessary, adjust timing, not temperature.

Continued

Alternate Method:

Same proportions as above. Take three cups of flour and make the dough soft enough to roll. Amalgamate the butter in the fourth cup of flour and proceed as above — same way — same folds.

Note: Dampen the baking sheet with cold water. It is not necessary to use grease unless there is a filling in the paste that will touch the sheet.

Allumettes à la Reine   Queen's Match Sticks

puff pastry   Bechamel sauce
ground leftover chicken   salt, pepper, nutmeg

Roll the pastry and cut into pieces 4½ inches by 2 inches. Coat with a layer of the chicken purée mixed with the sauce and seasonings. Wet the edges of the allumette and press a piece of pastry the same size over it — pressing the wet edges with a fork to seal. Bake at 350° to 375° for 25 to 30 minutes. Serve warm.

Pâte à Choux   Cream Puff Paste

½ cup butter or margarine   salt and nutmeg
1 cup water   3 to 4 eggs
1 tbsp sugar   1 cup flour

Bring water and butter to a boil until the butter is completely melted and slowly add seasoning. Pour in all the flour at once. Beat vigorously for 1 to 2 minutes until it forms a ball and leaves the sides of the pan. Remove from heat. In center of dough, break an egg. Beat thoroughly before adding the next. The last egg will be absorbed more slowly (sometimes three eggs will suffice). The dough should be able to hold its shape.

Pâte à choux can be made into puff crackers and hors d'oeuvre. It can also be refrigerated and warmed slowly when needed, but it will not rise as much as when the dough is fresh.

Profiterolles au Chocolat   Small Cream Puff
                                          with Chocolate Sauce

Prepare Pâte à choux. Preheat oven to 400°. Drop paste of walnut-size pieces onto a lightly greased cookie sheet, using a teaspoon or pastry bag. Bake for 20 to 25 minutes. Turn off heat, and prick each puff with a pointed fork to allow steam to escape. Leave them in the oven with the door ajar for 10 to 15 minutes to allow the centers to dry out. Fill with one of the cream mixtures that follow. If you fill them with ice cream, be sure to leave in the freezer until ready to serve. Serve with warm or cold chocolate sauce.

Crème Pâtissière

Filling for Cream Puffs

1 ½ cups milk
¼ cup butter
3 egg yolks
⅓ cup flour

2 tbsps cognac or rum,
  or 1 tsp vanilla
½ cup sugar

Scald the milk. Beat the sugar and egg yolks until lemon in color and runs like a ribbon. Add a little milk and the flour. Mix well. Gradually add the rest of the hot milk, and place over heat in a double boiler. Stir with a small wire whip or wooden spoon. Continue to stir over heat (to cook flour) for 5 or 6 minutes. Remove from heat; add butter and flavoring. Let it cool before using. Stir once in a while to prevent skin from forming on the surface. This cream will keep a few days in the refrigerator, or can be frozen for 3 to 4 months. This amount will fill 14 or 15 cream puffs.

To fill cream puffs: place filling in a pastry bag with a plain tube. Make a small slit on the side of the puff and insert tube, and squeeze in the filling. Or, with a small spoon, remove the top of the puff, insert filling and replace top. Sprinkle with powdered sugar.

VARIATIONS:

Crème Chantilly
Add about 1 cup of whipped cream to completely cooled Crème Pâtissière. Use for pastry, desserts, petit fours. For a topping in puff pastry, add ½ cup sugar, 1 tsp vanilla to the whipped cream.

Crème Saint Honoré
Add two stiffly beaten egg whites to the Crème Pâtissière. Add the egg whites when the cream is hot, as this will set the whites. Stir them quickly. Use to fill cream puffs or cake.

Crème Bourdaloue
To the Crème Pâtissière, add ¼ cup unsalted butter, 1 jigger of kirsch and 1 tsp of almond extract. Good base for fruit.

Crème Frangipane
To the Crème Pâtissière, add ½ cup almond paste or powdered almond.

Fanchonnettes

1 ½ cups Crème Pâtissière (see *recipe*)
Pâte Sucrée
  ⅓ cup sugar
  1 cup flour
  1 egg
  6 tbsps butter
  ½ tsp vanilla

2 eggs, separated
1 cup ground walnuts
1 tsp almond extract
½ cup jam, any flavor
10″ quiche pan, lightly greased

Continued

Prepare Pâte Sucrée by working the flour with the butter and sugar until a fine powder. Add the egg and vanilla and work until a dough. Chill to roll or press into the pan with your hands. Beat the yolks into the Crème Pâtissière, along with the nuts, jam, and extract. Whip the whites and fold in. Pour the mixture into the pan. Place on a cookie sheet and bake in a preheated 350⁰ oven for 30 to 45 minutes, or until an inserted knife comes out clean. If the top should start to brown before it it done, place a piece of foil on top.

Pâte à Beignets   Fritter Batter

1 cup flour
¼ tsp salt
½ tsp cinnamon
⅓ cup milk

2 eggs, separated
2 extra egg whites
1 tbsp oil
3 tbsps sugar (if batter is for dessert fritters)

Sift together the flour, salt and cinnamon. Mix the egg yolks and the milk. Beat the 4 egg whites well.

Add the yolks and milk to the flour, then quickly add the well-beaten egg whites. Mix well, then add the oil and sugar.

Let the batter stand at room temperature at least 20 minutes or longer (1 to 2 hours if time permits).

Drop spoonfuls of the batter into hot fat, cooking until brown on all sides.

Croissants   Crescent Rolls

2 pkgs dry yeast (2 tbsps)
¼ cup lukewarm water
1 tsp sugar
4 cups flour

1½ cups warm milk
1 tsp salt
¾ lb butter
egg diluted with a little milk

Dissolve the yeast in lukewarm water with sugar. Stir in one cup of flour, shape into a ball, cut a cross on the top. Place it in a bowl and cover. Let it rise in a warm place (75 to 80⁰) until it is doubled in bulk. Add the remaining flour, the milk and the salt and mix well. Knead until the dough is smooth and elastic. Place the dough in a greased bowl, brush the top with butter, cover and let it rise in a warmed place until it doubles again.

Roll the dough into a rectangle ½ inch thick. If the butter is too hard, beat it with a rolling pin to soften it. Place the butter in the center of the dough and fold the dough to enclose the butter like a package, or roll the dough and fold into thirds. Roll and fold again into thirds. Place the dough first in a towel and then inside a plastic bag. Chill several hours or overnight. Roll and fold twice more and chill thoroughly for about one hour.

Roll out in a square and cut into triangles, ⅛ inch thick. Starting at the wide end of the triangles, roll each of them up and press slightly to seal the end. Curve the ends to shape as a crescent. Place them on a greased baking sheet and brush with eggs diluted with a little milk. Cover and let them rise until doubled.

Bake in a 400⁰ preheated oven for 5 minutes. Reduce the heat to 350⁰ and bake 10 to 12 minutes more, or until the crescents are golden brown.

English Muffins

1 cup milk	¼ cup lukewarm water
2 tbsps sugar	4 cups flour, all purpose
1 tsp salt	1 egg, well beaten
3 tbsps butter	white corn meal
1 envelope of yeast	

Soften yeast in ¼ cup lukewarm water. Scald 1 cup of milk with the sugar, salt, and butter added. Cool to lukewarm. Stir 2 cups of flour into the milk, mix well, and add the softened yeast and egg. Beat all thoroughly. Add about 2 more cups of flour, or enough to make a moderately soft dough. Turn dough onto a lightly floured board and knead until smooth and satiny. Put dough into a buttered bowl and butter the surface lightly. Cover with a towel. Let rise in a warm place for about an hour or until doubled in bulk.

Punch the dough down, and let it rest for 10 minutes. Sprinkle a board slightly with some corn meal and roll dough to a ¼ inch thickness. Cut into 3 inch rounds. Sprinkle surface with more cornmeal. Cover with a dry towel and let rise on the board for 45 minutes or until double in bulk.

Place the muffins on an ungreased heavy griddle or heavy iron skillet and cook slowly. Have the griddle hot at first, then reduce the heat to brown them slowly, 8 minutes on each side. Cool. Pull apart and toast when serving.

Langue de Chat   Cat's Tongue

2 egg whites	⅓ cup sugar
⅓ cup + 1 tbsp flour	1 tsp vanilla flavoring (or any other
¼ cup softened butter	you prefer)

This cookie derives its name from its shape. It is possible to purchase special tins for this paste, but using a pastry bag is just as satisfactory.

Beat the butter and sugar together thoroughly before adding the whites, one at a time, mixing well each time. Using a sifter, sift flour in, also a little at a time. Add vanilla (or flavoring) to the smooth batter.

Grease special mold and fill with paste *or* let paste stiffen in the refrigerator and use a pastry bag and a round tube. Pipe chilled mixture to make little strips about an inch apart so they do not run into each other while baking. Bake in a preheated 375⁰ oven for 7 to 8 minutes. The cookie will be brown around the edges and white in the center. If desired, when cookies have finished baking, wrap them around a pencil, one at a time, making them resemble cigarettes. You must do this before they cool as they become quite crisp.

Crêpes

for 16 to 18 crêpes

3 tbsps of flour
3 eggs separated
1/8 tsp salt
3 tbsps sugar*
*For dessert crêpes only

1/8 tsp vanilla or
  2 tbsps of rum or cognac
1/2 tsp cinnamon*
2/3 cup milk, mixed with 1/3 cup of water
2 tbsps melted butter or oil

This batter should be made in advance and allowed to stand at least 15 minutes before it is used.

Mix flour, salt and sugar together. Moisten flour with a little milk, add the egg yolks and the whites beaten slightly, add vanilla or liquor, cinnamon, the melted butter and the rest of the milk. Let it rest a while.

When ready to use, grease a hot skillet, 8 to 9 inches in diameter, with a little butter on a piece of absorbent paper. Pour in a small amount of dough, just enough to cover bottom of pan. Swirl pan around to spread dough evenly. Brown on the underside (when crêpes are ready to turn, bubbles form over the top and sides are brown), turn and brown the other side. Stack crêpes on an ovenware plate and keep warm.

Crêpes à Lorientaise

16 Crêpes
3/4 lb cooked crab meat
1 cup Sauce Velouté made from
  flour, butter, fish stock
1/2 cup sherry to season sauce

Crab and Mushroom Crêpes

1/4 lb mushroom caps and stems
  sautéed with garlic
2 yolks and 1/3 cup cream for
  enrichment of sauce
salt, pepper, and nutmeg
chopped parsley to garnish

Season the Sauce Velouté with sherry and with salt, pepper, and nutmeg. The sauce should cook thoroughly in a double boiler. Fold in the yolks and cream to enrich the sauce, and fold in the cooked crab meat. Fold crêpe around the sauced crab and arrange them in a circular ovenproof dish. Top with mushrooms sautéed with garlic and chopped parsley. Reheat before serving.

Gateau de Crêpes Florentine

Florentine Crêpes Cake

4 to 6 servings

Crêpe dough:
1 cup flour
2 cups milk
4 eggs
salt
1 tbsp melted butter or oil
2 lbs spinach
1/4 cup butter

salt, pepper, nutmeg
1/4 cup cheese
1/2 cup rice
1 cup bouillon
1 green onion, chopped
Parmesan cheese
butter

Wash the spinach and blanch in boiling water 7 to 10 minutes. Drain, squeeze dry, and chop coarsely. Melt the butter and add it to the spinach. Stir in the salt, pepper, nutmeg, and cheese.

Meanwhile, prepare the crêpes as follows: put the flour in a bowl, add the eggs, milk, a little salt, and the butter or oil. Mix and let the batter rest 10 minutes. Prepare crêpes the size of a dessert plate.

Prepare the rice: sauté the green onion in butter, add the rice and bouillon and simmer for 17 to 20 minutes.

To assemble, lay a crêpe on a platter, put a layer of spinach on it, lay another crêpe on and cover with a layer or rice, and so on until all is used. Finish with a crêpe on top. Sprinkle with Parmesan cheese, dot with butter and put under the broiler to brown. Serve hot.

SALADS

Salads

In my method of cooking, it is not the cooking that takes time but the preparation. I always plan the meal and do all the preparation first ~ washing and slicing the vegetables, making the sauces or pastry ahead of time, so that the actual cooking is simple. When I worked for Mrs. Tobin, the whole week's menu was planned in advance. For her, I did all the planning and the shopping. After breakfast every day I would go to the market, from about nine o'clock to eleven o'clock, and I would check all the markets, looking for the best quality foods and buying the cheapest. That's how I shop today, always looking first at the quality because that is very important.

Between shopping, preparing and cooking, I worked very long hours. I would work from seven o'clock in the morning to eight o'clock at night. Sometimes I worked even crazier hours, especially when I cooked for Lily Pons. She would perform at the War Memorial Opera House and would then hold dinner parties afterward. I went to her hotel at midnight to prepare the dinner. When she was in town, I did all her work. Her washing, her ironing, her cooking. Charles and I lived on Mason Street so I could walk the one block to her apartment at the Huntington Hotel on Nob Hill. I didn't mind, really ~ she was a wonderful woman, and at her dinner parties I always met interesting, creative personalities from around the world. One of the most charming men I ever met was her husband (at the time), André Kostelanez.

Whenever Miss Pons was coming to town, she'd always wire or telephone to see if I was available. One year, when I couldn't cook for her because I was engaged elsewhere, I arranged for my cousin to help her out. They got along fine, too.

In my day there was no end to eating at a formal dinner. We didn't have too many appetizers or cocktails because the French didn't drink hard liquor. It was always Dubonnet, Vermouth, Sherry, or Port wine. There was also another entrée beside the main course. Salad was always eaten last, either with or without cheese, and then we had the dessert. But we never would serve a green salad as the first course. It would come after the meal and it would be a composed salad ~ such as shrimp or crabmeat salad, arranged with vegetables or fruit.

Things are different now. America has gone to France and France has come to America! Now Americans eat things like sweetbreads and French-style foods that they would never have eaten before.

Salade de Riz au Crabe

Crab and Rice Salad
6 servings

2 cups rice, cooked
½ lb crabmeat
1 cup black olives, pitted
½ cup pimento, chopped
1 tbsp mayonnaise
Olive oil (preferred)
salt, pepper

French dressing:
3 tbsps oil,
1 tbsp vinegar
1 tsp mustard (Dijon preferred)
few drops Worcestershire
salt, pepper
chives or green part of
    scallions (chopped)

Prepare 1 recipe of French dressing and stir into the cooked rice. Prepare another recipe of the French dressing with the addition of the mayonnaise and mix with the crab. Coat the olives with a little of the oil and add to the rice along with the crab and pimento. Check seasonings and serve.

Vinaigrette French dressing

(see also Sauces)

1½ cups oil
½ cup vinegar
¾ tsp salt
½ tsp pepper

1 tbsp prepared mustard (Dijon)
1 tsp Worcestershire sauce
1 clove garlic, crushed

This dressing is used in many salad recipes. For variations, see Sauces.

Les Délices de l'Eté

Summer Delight Salad
6 servings

6 to 7 Belgian endives
16 oz cream cheese
8 oz cottage cheese
1 cup chopped nuts,
    10 oz approx.
        fresh gooseberries, blueberries
        or strawberries

1 egg
3 tbsps oil
1 tbsp vinegar
salt and pepper
½ pint sour cream
1 tbsp paprika
chopped parsley, chives
    or tarragon

Remove a few outer leaves from endives and arrange them on a plate with ends touching in center for form a star. Cream the two cheeses together thoroughly, fold in nuts and chill. When almost ready to serve, add the berries. Beat egg with oil and vinegar until slightly thick. Season with salt and pepper. Mix in sour cream and paprika thoroughly and set aside.

To serve, mound cheese and berry mixture on top of star. Cut endives lengthwise and set them upright against the cheese. Spoon some of the sour cream dressing over the salad, sprinkle with parsley and top with a berry. Serve cold, with the remaining sauce offered separately.

Salade Carottes Rapés aux Raisins Frais et Bananes
Grated Carrots with Fresh Grapes and Bananas

6 servings

5 large carrots	½ cup fresh grapes
2 large bananas	1 tsp mustard
juice of 1 lemon	salt and pepper
3 tbsps oil	chopped parsley or tarragon

Peel, wash and dry carrots. Grate and season with lemon, mustard, oil, salt and pepper and some of the herbs. Add grapes and bananas; toss and serve on a bed of watercress or other greens. Sprinkle with more herbs.

Salade Normande   Normandy Salad

6 servings

1 lb butter beans (string yellow)	6 small onions
2 apples cut in small dices or coarsely grated	½ cup diced camembert or gruyere cheese
2 tbsps fresh cream (heavy) or sour cream	1 tbsp capers
3 tbsps oil	juice of 1 lemon or equal part of wine vinegar
1 clove garlic	1 tsp mustard (prepared)
1 tbsp chopped herbs (such as tarragon, chervil, basil, or parsley)	salt and pepper

Pare, wash and blanch the beans in boiling water for 15 to 20 minutes (do not put salt in the water until vegetables have come to a boil); drain. If onions are too big, cut in quarters. Prepare sauce in the bottom of salad bowl, combining the lemon juice, oil and mustard. Add the beans to the bowl with the onions, cheese, apples, cream, capers, chopped garlic and half of the herbs. Toss well before serving. Top with remaining herbs.

Salade du Morbihan   Morbihan Brittany Salad

6 servings

2 large tomatoes	4 zucchinis
6 artichoke bottoms	3-hard-cooked eggs
¼ lb. shrimps	

Cut the zucchinis in dices (do not peel). Blanch them in boiling water for 5 minutes. When they are cooled, add them to the tomatoes (cut in quarters), shrimp and artichokes. Season with French dressing and set on a bed of watercress or other greens. Arrange additional tomato and egg slices around the salad and serve with additional dressing in sauce boat.

Salade de Plougastel

Plougastel Salad
6 servings

1 escarole, romaine or
   lettuce
10 or 12 large strawberries
1 tbsp fine herbs,
   (parsley, chives, tarragon
   or chervil, or the combination of two)

1 bunch of radishes
2 oranges
2 hard-cooked eggs
Dressing:
3 tbsps of oil
1 tbsp of vinegar
1 tsp of mustard
few drops of tabasco sauce or
   worcestershire sauce

Wash salad carefully, drain and dry, cut it (in *chiffonade*) sliced fine, cut radishes in slices, cut oranges in slices (take all white out). Mix dressing in salad bowl, add all ingredients above with half the herbs, toss well, decorate top with the fresh strawberries and stuffed eggs of your choice. *Serve cold.* If not ready to serve, do not mix until last minute. Top with remaining herbs.

Salade Dubarry

Cauliflower Salad
8 servings

½ cup cream
½ lb cream cheese (8 oz)
¼ lb Roquefort (4 oz)
2 eggs, separated
2 eggs, hard-boiled
pinch of salt
pepper
nutmeg
paprika
1 env gelatin
4 thin slices ham
2 sour pickles

1 small jar caviar
4 crêpes (see Crêpes)
2 tsp chopped parsley
1 cauliflower, undercooked
4 slices smoked salmon
a vinaigrette sauce
chopped green onions
mustard
mayonnaise
more parsley
ketchup
1 greased ring mold

Put cream in blender with the cheeses, add parsley, salt, pepper, paprika and nutmeg, then add egg yolks.

Beat 2 whites stiffly and add to above, add dissolved gelatin and mix well. Pour half of mixture in greased ring mold. Cut the pickles in half and roll each slice of ham around each half pickle, then cut each roll of ham in half (to make 8).

Put caviar evenly in crêpes and roll each crêpe; cut in half. Trim the rolls if necessary to fit evenly in the mold, laying them alternately with the ham rolls on top of the cheese mixture.

Pour rest of cheese mixture into mold and refrigerate. Cook cauliflower, it should be quite firm (or it can be served raw), and marinate in a vinaigrette sauce with chopped green onions. This goes in the middle of the ring mold.

Hard boil 2 eggs, mince them or put them through a sieve. Add mustard, mayonnaise, salt, pepper, parsley to make a paste. Dip the slices of smoked salmon in this, and arrange around the mold. Coat salmon with mayonnaise mixed with some ketchup.

Chou-Fleur Rapé au Thon

Grated Cauliflower with Tuna Fish

1 cauliflower
french dressing
1 small can tuna fish
salt and pepper
1 lemon

fines herbs:
   chervil, tarragon, basil,
   chives
lettuce leaves

Grate the cauliflower, sprinkle with lemon juice. In the meantime crumble the tuna fish seasoned with French dressing and herbs, reserving some for top. Mix tuna and herbs with cauliflower, serve in a salad bowl lined with lettuce. Sprinkle with more herbs.

Chou-Fleur au Fromage

Cauliflower Salad with Cheese

1 cauliflower head
lemon juice
3 tbsps oil
1 tbsp vinegar

¼ lb roquefort cheese
1 tsp mustard
chopped chives and parsley
salt and pepper

Cut cauliflower in small flowerets. Sprinkle them with lemon juice. Prepare the vinaigrette with 3 tbsps oil, 1 tbsp vinegar, 1 tsp of mustard, salt and pepper. Crumble the cheese and mix well with the vinaigrette, toss the cauliflower in and sprinkle with chives and parsley.

 HINT:

Never rinse wine or sherry bottles. Use them for storing oil, as the alcohol helps prevent rancidity.

Laitue Farcie

Stuffed Lettuce
6 servings

6 hearts lettuce
6 slices ham
1 cup chicken meat, cooked
6 small white onions
1 tbsp tarragon
1 pkg unflavored gelatin
6 hard-cooked eggs
salt and pepper

1½ cups hot bouillon
¹/₃ cup sherry
juice of 1 lemon
3 tbsps oil
1 cup mayonnaise (homemade,
 if possible)
4 medium tomatoes

Wash and drain the hearts of lettuce and open the leaves very carefully. To prepare the stuffing, cut ham finely with the tarragon and the chicken. Dissolve gelatin in small amount of cold water and pour over the hot bouillon, stirring well and adding the sherry. Let it cool a little and add ½ cup to the ham and chicken mixture; season with the oil and lemon, salt and pepper.

Stuff the leaves of lettuce with this mixture, and serve on bed of watercress or other greens. Arrange tomatoes and eggs and onions around, and garnish with chopped leftover meat jelly (if you have any). Serve with a bowl of mayonnaise or French dressing and you have a wonderful first course or luncheon dish.

Salade Alsacienne
6 to 8 servings

French dressing: (see Sauces)
3 to 4 oz sauerkraut
few leaves lettuce,
 coarse shredded
chopped parsley

½ lb garlic sausage, boiled
 skinned, sliced thin
4 oz hard cheese (Swiss, etc.)
1 6 to 8 oz can of tuna
 (packed in oil preferred)

Garnish: Fresh grated cheese, chopped parsley, lettuce leaves, and sliced green of scallions.

Prepare French dressing. Salt and pepper to taste. Mix well and add salad ingredients; toss thoroughly to coat with dressing.

Note: When adding tuna, include all the oil it is packed in.

To serve: Line platter with lettuce leaves and pile salad in the center. Sprinkle with the grated cheese, parsley and sliced green of scallions.

Aspic de Légumes

Vegetable Salad in Aspic
8 servings

2 lbs carrots, diced
1 medium potato, diced
½ lb green beans
1 lb fresh peas or
 1 pkg frozen
2 slices green pepper

1½ cups chicken broth or
 consommé
french dressing (see Sauces)
1 tbsp chopped herbs;
 chives, parsley and tarragon
1 env gelatin

Cook all vegetables separately in boiling water, adding 1 tsp salt and then simmering for 15 to 20 minutes. Drain. While gelatin dissolves in ¼ cup cold water, bring chicken broth to a boil. Stir in gelatin and continue to cook until completely melted. Cool the mixture until syrupy and just beginning to jell. Then pour a little into mold to cover bottom and let set. Mix the French dressing well with the cooked vegetables and marinate for at least 2 hours.

With a few slices of carrot and green pepper, decorate the bottom of the mold, then pour over a little more of the jelly to hold vegetables in place. When this is set spoon all vegetables into the mold and add remaining jelly. Place in refrigerator to jell.

To unmold, dip in very hot water briefly, then invert aspic onto a platter. Decorate with chopped jelly or watercress and serve with additional vinaigrette.

Tomates Farcies Gabrielle

Stuffed Tomatoes
6 servings

6 medium tomatoes, washed
and dried
½ cup mayonnaise, well
seasoned with Dijon
mustard
½ tsp salt
pepper and paprika to taste

1 avocado, diced
juice of ½ lemon
6½ oz can of tuna
1½ tbsp parsley, chopped
lettuce or watercress
leaves

Cut off tomato tops and remove pulp. Turn tomatoes upside down on a plate or towel and let dry. Season mayonnaise with salt, pepper and paprika. Add the avocado sprinkled with lemon juice along with tuna and 1 tbsp chopped parsley. Fill tomatoes with this mixture, sprinkle with remaining parsley and serve very cold on a bed of lettuce leaves.

Bordure de Concombre

Cucumber Ring
6 to 8 servings

3 large cucumbers
1 cup diced celery
½ tsp salt
¼ tsp pepper, freshly ground
2 pkgs lime-flavored gelatin,
or 1 pkg lime jello

fines-herbes: chopped
tarragon, chives, chervil,
fennel or dill, 1 tbsp in all
¼ cup vinegar
½ cup water
1½ extra cups water

Peel cucumbers and reduce to a pulp, take seeds out if too big. Dissolve gelatin in ½ cup of cold water. Bring 1 cup of water to a boil, add gelatin or jello stirring until completely dissolved; add salt, pepper, vinegar and herbs, celery and cucumber pulp.

Fill a ring mold and chill.

Salade de Homard en Bordure

Lobster Salad in Ring

6 to 8 servings

meat from 2 lobsters
3 hard-cooked eggs
2 tbsps chopped celery
1 tsp chives
1 tsp chopped fennel or dill
1 tsp chopped parsley

2 tbsps lemon juice
1 tsp Dijon mustard
¼ cup mayonnaise
salt and pepper to taste
few drops Worcestershire
  sauce

Cut lobster in dices; chop the eggs. Thin the mayonnaise with lemon juice, mustard, salt and pepper and Worcestershire sauce.

Mix lobster, eggs, celery, herbs in the sauce; fill ring and serve cold.

Poinsettia Salad

This festive salad has three layers prepared in three separate molds of graduated sizes. These are unmolded and served together with both a French dressing and a sour cream-mayonnaise dressing.

1st layer: largest flat-bottomed bowl or dish
            2 cucumbers and 1 bunch fresh spinach chopped in blender
            1 envelope gelatin dissolved in 2 cups liquid
            1 green onion chopped
            a little lemon juice
            salt and pepper

2nd layer: smaller flat-bottomed bowl or dish
            3 cups fresh tomatoes, puréed with a few green onions and parsley
            1 envelope gelatin dissolved in a little lemon juice
            salt and pepper

3rd layer: smallest flat-bottomed bowl or dish
            1 oz package cream cheese, whipped
            Worcestershire sauce
            salt and pepper
            nutmeg and chives to taste
            blue cheese (optional)
            2 egg whites, beaten
            1 envelope gelatin, dissolved in a little liquid

Unmold in the above order on a large platter. Decorate with a flower on the top, using a scallion (dipped in boiling water) for the stem and leaves; pimento slices for petals; and sieved egg yolk for the center. Frame salad with escarole.

Serve with a French dressing with capers and hard-cooked egg yolks (sieved) added, and a dressing made of equal parts sour cream and mayonnaise. Dressings are served separately.

DESSERTS

Desserts

Le crêpe de Grandmère is the best in the world ~ I make mine very, very thin ~ like paper, not soggy and anemic like the ones I've seen here.

Congressman Frank Havner used to celebrate his birthday every year by having dinner at my house. One year he brought his secretary, Madeleine, with him. Bimbo, the San Francisco restaurateur, was there also with his wife. I fixed them a wonderful meal, but afterward, Madeleine said to me, "Josephine, I was expecting you to fix crêpes Suzette." I explained to her that I thought the dinner was very rich, and as Frank was no longer a young man, he didn't need a rich dessert too.

Bimbo spoke up and said, "How about going to my restaurant and making them overe there?" I said, "Is that a challenge or an order?" and he said, "Both!"

So off we went to Bimbo's on Columbus Avenue ~ it was already after midnight. When we got there, Bimbo told me to go into the kitchen and have the chef get the pancakes and anything else that I needed. So I went into the kitchen and asked the chef, who showed me the pancakes ~ they weren't crêpes, they were flapjacks! I went back into the dining room and told Bimbo I wasn't going to serve my Suzette on flapjacks! We decided I would make my own crêpes, so back into the kitchen I went, and had the chef help me because it was already so late.

When we finally brought them to the table everyone was so happy, that they asked me what I would like to drink. I said, "Champagne!" So we finished the dinner with Möet et Chandon champagne and crêpes Suzette at three o'clock in the morning.

Note: For basic crêpe recipe and entrée crêpes see Section on Pastry Doughs, Bread and Crêpes.

Les Crêpes de Grandmère

1 recipe crêpes
4 oz Philadelphia cream cheese
¼ cup sugar
rind (zest) of ½ lemon,
    chopped fine

Crêpes with Cream Cheese
Filling for 16 to 18 crêpes

juice of ½ lemon
1 tsp vanilla
1 egg yolk
3 tbsps sour cream
1 tbsp raisins

Mix the cream cheese with all remaining ingredients to form a soft cream. Fill the crêpes, roll and warm. Dust them with powdered sugar before serving.

Crêpes au Miel

1 recipe of crêpes
½ cup honey

Crêpes with Honey Butter and Orange
6 to 8 servings

½ stick sweet butter
juice of ½ lemon
grated rind of 1 to 2 oranges

Stack the crêpes, sprinkling orange rind on every 6 to 8 crêpes. Cut the stack into sections like a cake.

Melt the honey and butter together, add remaining ingredients. Pour over the crêpes and serve.

Crêpes Quimperoise

Buckwheat crêpes
4 tbsps buckwheat flour
3 eggs
²/₃ cup water
¹/₃ cup milk

Crepes with Chocolate Sauce
16 to 18 crêpes

Chocolate Sauce
3 yolks
¹/₃ cup sugar
1 cup strong coffee
    (2 tbsps instant: 1 cup water)
½ lb semi-sweet chocolate
1 tsp cornstarch
½ cup cognac (or to taste)
¹/₃ cup cream
sweet butter

Melt chocolate in top of double boiler with the coffee. Mix the yolks with the sugar. Slowly stir in the chocolate mixture. Add the cornstarch and return to double boiler. Stir until mixture thickens. Add cream and cognac just before serving.

Prepare crêpes. Smear each crêpe with the sweet butter and fold into quarters. Overlap on a round serving platter. Pour chocolate sauce over. Serve warm.

Crêpe Suzette

Filling for 16 to 18 crêpes

1 recipe of crêpes
3 egg yolks
½ cup sugar
1 cup orange juice

¼ cup sweet butter, softened
Curaçao (to taste)
grated rind (zest) of 1 orange
brandy

Mix the egg yolks and sugar. Boil the orange juice and pour it over. Cook slowly, stirring, until the mixture is like custard. Cool to lukewarm, then beat the mixture into softened butter. Add Curaçao to taste. Add the grated orange peel. (At this point the mixture may be frozen for later use.)

Butter each crêpe with the orange butter and fold into quarters. Arrange them on a flame-proof dish. Sprinkle liberally with brandy, cover with foil, and heat in the oven. When ready to serve, heat additional brandy in a small saucepan. Ignite and pour, flaming, over the crêpes.

First Method:
Créme au Beurre Suzette

Suzette Cream Filling

6 servings

1 cup orange juice and rind
4 egg yolks
½ cup sugar

½ lb unsalted butter
1 liqueur glass Curaçao
1 liqueur glass cognac (large)

Warm the orange juice in a double boiler. Beat egg yolks with sugar until lemon colored and thick. Pour hot orange juice over the yolks, little by little, and stir; return to double boiler and stir constantly until the mixture becomes creamy and coats the wooden spoon. Let it cool to lukewarm. Beat this mixture with ½ lb softened butter, add orange rind and Curaçao.

Fill the pancakes, folding in four like a handkerchief, and arrange pancakes in a fireproof glass pie plate and then put them in the oven to warm with a cover on top. Warm cognac a little, pour over pancakes and ignite. Serve at once.

Second Method:
Créme au Beurre Suzette

Suzette Cream Filling

¼ lb butter
1 cup orange juice
   and rind

1 liqueur glass Curaçao
½ cup sugar
1 large liqueur glass cognac

Continued

Melt butter, add sugar and let cook until sugar has caramelized a little. Add orange juice and rind and Curaçao. Dip pancake in this mixture and fold it in four. Ignite with warm cognac. Serve hot.

Soufflé Glacé au Citron   Cold Lemon Soufflé

juice of 4 lemons,   ¾ cup sugar
  the rinds of 2   4 eggs, separated
½ cup sweet butter $^1/_3$ cup water

Beat the egg yolks with ¼ cup sugar, add warm lemon juice and rind and cook over hot water until creamy. When still warm, beat in sweet butter and then the egg whites beaten stiff with ½ cup sugar. Grease a soufflé mold on the *outside* and wrap waxed paper or aluminum foil around it about two inches above the border. (This gives the impression of a hot soufflé rising above the mold). Fill with lemon mixture and chill. When ready to serve, remove the paper or aluminum foil and clean the butter from the mold with a damp cloth.

Grand Marnier Soufflé

4 tbsps butter $^1/_3$ cup sugar
$^1/_3$ cup flour   1 jigger Curaçao or Triple Sec
1 cup fresh orange juice,   10 egg whites
  warmed   pinch of salt
6 egg yolks   ¼ to ½ cup Grand Marnier
1 to 2 tsps orange rind

Preheat oven to 350º.
Grease a 2-qt soufflé dish and dust with sugar.
Melt butter in double boiler, add flour and cook the **bouillie** a few minutes. Gradually stir in orange juice and cook until mixture is quite thick. Remove from heat and add egg yolks, one at a time, stirring after each. Add orange rind along with sugar and Curaçao.
Beat egg whites until foamy, add salt and continue to beat until stiff. Fold bouillie into whites and add Grand Marnier. Place mixture in soufflé dish. Using a knife, make a circular incision near the edge of the dish to allow the soufflé to rise better.
Place dish in preheated oven in a pan of warm water and bake for 20 to 30 minutes.

Note: In varying proportions, be sure to add 1 tsp flour for each egg.

Soufflé aux Fraises   ## Strawberry Soufflé

2 to 3 baskets fresh
   strawberries of 2 or 3 pkgs
   frozen (saving the juice)
¾ cup sugar if strawberries
   are fresh (½ cup if frozen)
½ tsp cream of tartar
1 six-cup soufflé mold,
   pyrex dish or charlotte mold;
   butter and sugar to coat mold.

2 tbsps corn starch, arrowroot,
   or potato starch
4 egg whites
one cup sugar
1 cup water
dash of salt

Preheat oven to 400⁰.

Crush and purée the strawberries, enough to make 1¾ to 2 cups. Set aside. Butter and sugar the mold. Boil water and sugar, stir until dissolved, then reduce heat and cover, boiling gently for 7 to 10 minutes, until it bubbles. With a teaspoon, take a little out and drop it in cold water — if it forms a soft ball between the fingers, the syrup is ready.

While the syrup is in the making, beat the egg whites until foamy, then add salt and cream of tartar. Pour hot syrup over egg whites very slowly while continuing to beat until all is absorbed. Fold in corn starch (or other) very gently, cutting through center or sides and bottom, turning bowl as you fold, in order to mix well without deflating. Add strawberry purée and fold again. (If you wish, you can put a collar around mold, but it isn't necessary. Fruit soufflés never rise too high.) Pour strawberry mixture into buttered mold ¾ full, and bake 20 to 25 minutes at 375⁰, on a lower oven level. Serve immediately with a strawberry or raspberry sauce or whipped cream. The juice of the fruit can be thickened with a little cornstarch to make a sauce.

Note: Fruit soufflés deflate very quickly, so try to serve immediately.

Soufflé Glacé aux Fraises en Surprise S.S. France
Soufflé with Strawberry Surprise
12 servings

1½ cup sugar
⅛ tsp salt
6 egg yolks
1 tbsp Grand Marnier
1 pt strawberries
1 qt heavy cream
2 tsps vanilla extract
½ cup heavy cream

Sauce:
1 pt strawberries
⅓ cup sugar
3 tbsps Grand Marnier

Make a collar with foil and tie collar with a string 3 inches above top of 1-qt soufflé dish.

In a saucepan, combine 1½ cups sugar with ⅔ cup water over low heat,

Continued

stirring until sugar is dissolved. Increase heat to medium and bring syrup to a boil. Boil to 230⁰ on a candy thermometer or until a little syrup forms a 2-inch thread when dropped from spoon.

Meanwhile, in a medium bowl, with an electric mixer at medium speed, beat yolks and salt until light. Pour hot syrup in a thin stream into egg mixture, beating constantly. Continue beating 8 to 10 minutes or until mixture begins to cool. Refrigerate, covered, for 30 minutes.

Wash 1 pt of strawberries, drain and hull. Crush enough to make ½ cup. Cut the rest in half in a small bowl and toss with 1 tbsp Grand Marnier. Refrigerate.

In a chilled large bowl, beat 1 qt heavy cream with the vanilla until stiff. Gently fold in crushed strawberries and cooled egg mixture. Make sure it is well combined. Turn into prepared soufflé dish and freeze overnight.

The next day, whip ½ cup cream until stiff. Place in pastry bag with star tip and refrigerate.

Sauce: Wash strawberries, drain and hull. Cut in half and place in small bowl. Add sugar and liqueur. Mix well. Refrigerate.

Remove foil collar from soufflé dish. With a heated sharp knife, cut around top of soufflé, about ½" from edge and about 1" deep. Then cut inside circle into quarters. Cut under each quarter and remove it in one piece and place on a cookie sheet in the freezer.

Scoop out enough of the soufflé to make space for the strawberries that were prepared the previous day. Fill cavity with the berries and replace the soufflé quarters. With the whipped cream in the pastry bag, cover the cuts and decorate the top.

Serve at once, or soufflé can be returned to the freezer until serving time, preferably no longer than 30 minutes. Serve with sauce.

Soufflé Glacé aux Apricots   Apricot Iced Soufflé

1 lb ripe apricots
3 egg whites
1 cup sugar
1 tsp vanilla

juice of 1 lemon
½ pt whipped cream
1 cup water

Boil water and sugar, stir until dissolved, then reduce heat and cover, boiling gently for 7 to 10 minutes, until it bubbles. With a spoon, take a little out and drop it in cold water and if it forms a soft ball between the fingers, the syrup is ready.

While waiting for the syrup, stone, peel and mash the apricots to a pulp (you can use an electric mixer). Beat the egg whites very stiff, adding to them the hot syrup very slowly, continuing to beat until all is absorbed. Continue beating until almost cold, then add the purée of apricot.

Whip the cream and add to the apricot-egg mixture. Grease the outside of the mold with butter and make collar with waxed paper or tin foil all around, 2" high, fastened with string; pour mixture into mold and freeze for at least 2 hours.

Before serving, take paper collar off and wipe the butter off the outside of the mold. Sprinkle with confectioners sugar. It should rise above the mold 1 or 2″, to give the impression of a real soufflé.

Mousse aux Mandarines

Mandarin Orange Mousse

¹/₃ cup fresh or canned
   mandarin orange juice or
   orange juice
2 skins of whole mandarin
   oranges or more, finely
   chopped
lady fingers dipped in liqueur
   (optional)
2 or 3 mandarin oranges or
   other citrus fruit

1 cup sugar
3 egg yolks
3 egg whites
¾ cup butter or sweet
   margarine
2 tbsps Curaçao, Cointreau, Triple
   Sec, or Grand Marnier
whipped cream

Put sugar and juice in heavy saucepan. Boil until soft ball stage: syrup will barely drop from spoon.

Beat yolks with wooden spoon, pour in hot syrup slowly. Stir on low flame until thick. Do not add all the syrup before heating with yolks. Add rest of syrup after yolks are thick. Stir in soft butter 2 tbsps at a time. Add liqueur and chopped skin. Beat whites of egg until stiff adding a little salt. Fold into yolk mixture. Refrigerate 4 to 5 hours or freeze after pouring into greased mold. Unmold and decorate platter with mandarin slices and whipped cream.

Mousse au Chocolat

Chocolate Mousse

lady fingers or stale
   sponge cake
12 to 16 oz. semi-sweet
   chocolate
½ cup Curaçao or Cointreau
3 to 4 egg yolks
4 tbsps strong coffee
¹₃ cup sugar
½ cup unsalted butter
3 egg whites, beaten stiff
¾ cup heavy cream, whipped
a Charlotte mold or similar

Finishing touch:
¾ cup heavy cream, whipped
¼ cup confectioners sugar
2 tbsps Curaçao or Cointreau
chocolate curls and
   shaved chocolate

Line the bottom and sides of mold with lady fingers or sponge cake. Sprinkle with liqueur. Set aside.

In the top of a double boiler, set over simmering water, melt the chocolate

Continued

with the coffee. With an electric mixer, beat eggs slightly. Beat in the chocolate mixture and 3 tbsps liqueur. Blend well at moderate speed. Fold in egg whites. When cool, fold in whipped cream. Pour the mousse into the prepared mold and chill. After one hour, cover top of mousse with more cake or lady fingers and press down slightly. Sprinkle with remaining liqueur and chill again for a few hours or overnight.

Just before serving, whip 1¼ cups heavy cream with ¼ cup confectioners sugar and 2 tbsps liqueur. Run a knife around the sides of the mold to loosen the mousse and invert it onto a serving platter. Cover the cake, top and sides, with the whipped cream, using a pastry bag fitted with a fancy tube to pipe rosettes on top with the remaining cream. Decorate the top with chocolate curls and the sides with shaved chocolate. Serve with a coffee custard cream.

Note: To freeze: cover mousse tightly. It will keep several months.

 HINT:

Whites of eggs can be stored in a jar. Measure out for cooking by shaking the jar and pouring slowly — the whites will pour out separately. Egg whites can be frozen for longer storage, or kept in the refrigerator.

Petits Pots de Crème au Chocolat

4 squares semi-sweet baker's
   chocolate
4 egg yolks
5 egg whites

4 tbsps sugar
¼ cup *sweet* butter or
   unsalted margarine

Melt chocolate, butter and sugar in double boiler. While still warm, add the 4 egg yolks and the 5 egg whites beaten stiff. Pour into little crocks, set in ice box for a couple of hours and serve in their crocks.

Pots de Crème au Cafe   Coffee Custard Cups

4 eggs
3 yolks
3½ cups milk

1 tbsp instant coffee
   diluted in milk
½ cup sugar

Preheat oven to 300⁰.

Beat eggs and sugar until light and foamy. Gradually pour in hot milk while beating. Strain mixture and fill custard cups. Set custard cups in a pan of hot water. (Water should reach the halfway mark of custard cups.) To ensure a smooth custard, regulate heat so water never comes to a boil. Bake for 35 to 40 minutes. Custard is done when a knife plunged down comes out clean.

Oeuf a la Reine

Custard with Meringue

6 servings

1 cup milk, heated
1 cup sugar
4 oz heavy cream, whipped
1 tbsp gelatin
salt

3 eggs, separated
1 tsp vanilla
1 to 2 tbsps flavoring:
    vanilla, kirsch, etc.
2 cups crushed strawberries,
    mixed with ¼ cup sugar

Stir yolks with ½ cup sugar. Slowly stir in the heated milk. Place mixture over heat (preferably in top of double boiler) and stir until thickens. Soften gelatin in a little cold water and stir into the custard mixture, making sure it completely dissolves. Cool before adding the whipped cream. Add flavoring to taste. Set aside. Beat egg whites with a dash of salt. Beat in ½ cup sugar and the tsp of vanilla. Fill a shallow pan with water and heat until it is barely simmering. Drop a large tbsp of egg white mixture into the water and poach for three minutes on each side. Drain thoroughly.

To assemble: Pour some of the custard mixture into 1½ qt buttered casserole. Gently place some of the meringues around the bowl and continue to layer the meringues and the custard, ending with the custard. Chill until set. Unmold onto a serving platter and surround with the crushed berries that have been sweetened with sugar (kirsch may be added if desired) to taste.

Tarte au Citron

Lemon Pie

1 recipe of pâté brisèe
6 lemons
¾ cup water
¼ cup butter

3 egg yolks
2 egg whites
1 cup sugar
2 whole eggs

Preheat oven to 375⁰. Prepare a baked crust from the pâte brisèe.

Squeeze the juice of 3 lemons and add to the water. Beat the egg yolks and 2 whole eggs with the sugar and butter.

Bring the water and lemon juice to a boil and beat it into the egg mixture. (Beat in two egg whites stiff.) Pour the mixture into the precooked pie crust.

Slice the other 3 lemons and cook them in a light syrup until they are glazed. Garnish the pie with a circle of glazed lemon slices and bake at 375⁰ for 15 to 20 minutes.

Gâteau de Fromage
Cheese Cake
4 to 6 servings

Crust:
¾ cup cake crumbs
¼ cup butter
½ tsp cinnamon

Topping:
1 pt sour cream
3½ tbsps sugar
1 tsp vanilla

Filling:
12 oz cream cheese
2 tbsps sour cream
½ cup sugar
1 tsp cinnamon
1 tsp vanilla
1 lemon rind, finely chopped
2 tbsps lemon juice
3 eggs
1 pinch salt

Crust: Mix the crumbs with butter and cinnamon and press into the bottom and sides of a glass pie plate.

Filling: Mix all ingredients in order given. Pour this cheese mixture into the prepared crust and bake at 350⁰ for 25 minutes. Test with a knife (if it comes out dry, the filling is cooked). Remove from oven.

Topping: Mix sour cream with the sugar and vanilla. Spread over the top of the baked cake, then bake 5 minutes more.

Refrigerate for 5 hours before serving.

Gâteau Josephine
Liqueur Pie

1¼ cups crumbs: cookie, cake, graham cracker, etc.
4 tbsps melted butter (unsalted)
8 oz cream cheese
4 oz butter (unsalted)
1 cup sugar
2 cups heavy cream, whipped

½ cup flavoring:
Creme de Menthe,
Creme de Cafe,
Creme de Cocoa,
or any flavored liqueur
of your choice

Crust: Mix crumbs (set aside 1½ tbsps to sprinkle on top) with melted butter. Add a little sugar if a sweeter crust is desired. Using your fingers or the back of a spoon, press crumbs against the sides and bottom of a filmed 10"-12" pie dish.

Filling: With an electric beater, mix the butter and cream cheese and add the sugar. Slowly add the flavoring. Add the whipped cream and thoroughly mix. Pour into crust, sprinkle with the crumbs, and refrigerate. Serve chilled.

Tarte Charles

Apple Tart Charles

2 lbs apples
  (about 5 cups when sliced)
½ tsp cinnamon
5 oz jam: apricot, strawberry,
  currant jelly, etc.

½ cup sugar
2 ozs butter
pâté brisée

Preheat oven to 375⁰. Peel and core the apples. Cut in quarters and slice thin. Line an 8″ or 9″ pie plate with the pie dough. Prick the bottom with the tines of a fork. Precook the dough 15 minutes with a weight on it (beans, rice, or another smaller pie plate that will fit inside). Remove weight, place apples in precooked crust, sprinkling with sugar and cinnamon, and dot with butter. Cover with more pie dough and seal together. Glaze with one egg mixed with 1 tbsp water. Bake on a cookie sheet in a preheated oven for 1 hour and 15 minutes. If dough browns too quickly, cover with brown paper or tin foil. Remove from oven, cut a circle (about 2″ in diameter) from the top and pour half a jar of jam into the hole. Replace circle of crust and cut pie in wedges.

Tarte aux Poires

Pear Tart

1 lb pears
2 cups water
1 cup sugar
1 recipe pâte brisée

orange marmalade
juice of 1 lemon
roasted almonds, chopped
½ pt whipping cream

Preheat oven to 350⁰.

Poach the pears in a light syrup of 2 cups water and 1 cup sugar for 10 minutes. Allow them to cool.

Roll out the paste, line a pie plate with it, cover it with thin foil and put a weight on the foil (use peas, beans, rice, etc.). Bake for 15 minutes at 350⁰ to 375⁰. Remove the weight and the foil.

Spread a thin layer of orange marmalade on the bottom of the crust. Cut the poached pears into quarters and arrange them on the marmalade. Melt more orange marmalade with the juice of 1 lemon and glaze the pears with it. Sprinkle with chopped roasted almonds. Decorate with whipped cream.

Note: The syrup of the pears can be reduced until it forms a caramel and used instead of the marmalade to glaze the pears.

Gâteau Genoise

Genoise Cake

The genoise is a very finely textured cake. The method is to beat the eggs and sugar over warm water until the mixture is warm and thick, then to beat it away from the warm water at room temperature until it is a little cool and even thicker. It is a low-lying cake of 1½ to 2 inches, used for petit fours as

Continued

well as for layer cake. For petit fours, a square pan is generally used.

3 large eggs	rind of 1 lemon
½ cup sugar	¾ cup of flour
1 pinch salt	4 tbsps melted butter
1 tsp of vanilla	2 round cake pans

Preheat oven to 350⁰. Grease pan lightly and line bottom with waxed paper.

Beat eggs, sugar and salt over warm water (not hot) making sure the bowl does not touch the water. Beat until warm, foamy and thick. Scrape the sides occasionally so sugar can be well blended with the eggs; add vanilla and lemon rind. Remove bowl from over the warm water and beat a few minutes until it begins to cool. Sift the flour, adding 2 spoonsful at a time and alternately fold in 2 tbsps of the melted butter, being careful not to include any of the residue that has settled at the bottom of the pan. Repeat, adding flour and butter, then pour batter into prepared pans.

Bake in a preheated oven for 30 to 35 minutes or until tested with tooth pick that comes out clean. It is done when cake shows a line of shrinkage from the sides of the pan; remove cake from oven and let cool 5 to 10 minutes, then reverse onto a rack. If cake is not used right away, wrap it airtight (or it will dry out quickly), and refrigerate for several days or freeze for several months.

Gâteau Chantilly aux Cerises   Genoise Cake with Cherries

genoise cake	vanilla
1 pt whipping cream	¼ lb pitted cherries
⅓ cup sugar	kirsch (optional)

Make a genoise cake in 2 pans, one bigger than the other. Whip the cream; add the sugar and the vanilla to taste.

Slice each genoise horizontally, covering each layer entirely with whipped cream. Place the smaller one on top, also covering it with whipped cream. Finish with a fluted pastry tube filled with more whipped cream and decorate with as many cherries as desired. The cake may be sprinkled with kirsch.

Gateau Alsacien   Alsatian Coffee Cake

1 env dry active yeast	¼ cup sugar
1 cup of milk	¾ cup butter, softened
½ tsp salt	1 tsp vanilla or 3 tsps of rum
1 tsp grated lemon rind	2 cups sifted all-purpose flour
2 eggs	½ cup raisins
¼ cup chopped blanched almonds (optional)	¼ cup cut glazed mixed fruits (optional)
confectioners' sugar	

In a bowl put ½ cup flour, add the yeast, the warm milk (tepid) and mix well to obtain a soft paste, almost liquid. Over this mixture sift the rest of the flour without mixing. Cover with plastic and set in a warm place (75 to 80⁰) until the yeast raises and pierces through the dry flour on top.

To the dough, add the softened butter, beating a little at a time. Then add sugar and salt, beating well until the paste becomes elastic. Last add the raisins and the optional almonds and glazed fruits. Turn into a well-buttered mold and allow to rise double, almost to the top. Bake in a preheated oven (350⁰) for 40 to 45 minutes; let cool for 5 minutes and turn on a rack. Dust with powdered sugar.

Gateau de Potiron — Pumpkin Cake

6 to 8 servings

2 cups pumpkin meat, fresh
   or canned
½ cup ground almonds
½ cup cream
2 tbsps butter
2 egg yolks
1 whole egg

2 oz brandy
1 tbsp vanilla
¹/₃ cup sugar
1 tbsp flour
2 egg whites, beaten stiff
¹/₃ cup sugar for meringue
powdered sugar to sprinkle over

Preheat oven to 300⁰.

If using fresh pumpkin, cook in a little water and mash. Add the almonds, cream, butter, egg yolks, whole egg, brandy, vanilla, ¹/₃ cup sugar and the flour to the pumpkin and mix well. Put the mixture in a buttered ovenproof dish and set in the oven for 45 minutes.

Beat the 2 egg whites until stiff, add ¹/₃ cup sugar slowly, while beating, to make meringue. Spread the meringue over the pumpkin mixture and put back in the oven a few minutes to brown.

Serve cold, sprinkled with powdered sugar.

Soupe a l'Anglaise — English Trifle

1 lb of sponge cake
strawberry jam or currant
   jelly
chopped walnuts or almonds
heavy cream, whipped
rum

Custard Cream:
1 cup milk
4 egg yolks
½ cup sugar
½ tsp vanilla

Prepare custard cream by scalding milk. Beat egg yolks with sugar until lemon color and add the hot milk, slowly. Cook in top of double boiler, over medium heat, until mixture coats the spoon. Add vanilla and let cool.

Line any type dish desired with slices of cake. Sprinkle slices with rum.

Continued

smear on the jam or jelly, then sprinkle on the chopped nuts. Repeat the layers of cake and jam, then pour the custard cream over all. Top with whipped cream and dot here and there with jam or jelly. The jam can be omitted and the custard cream used between layers instead of pouring it all over at once.

Truffettes   *Makes 18 truffettes*

¼ lb semi-sweet chocolate
¼ cup sweet butter
3 tbsps milk

1 egg yolk, beaten
powdered or grated
  chocolate

Over simmering water slowly melt the semi-sweet chocolate with the milk, stirring constantly; add the butter and stir until blended. Cool the mixture a little, then stir in the egg yolk and chill the mixture until firm.

Form small balls, about half the size of a walnut, and roll them in powdered or grated chocolate. Store the truffettes in the refrigerator.

Soupirs de Nonnes   ## Nuns' Sighs

1 cup water
¼ cup butter
½ tsp salt
1 tsp sugar

1 cup flour
4 eggs
flavoring: lemon, vanilla, rum, etc.
deep fat for frying

Put the water, butter, salt and sugar in a saucepan and bring to a boil. When the butter has melted completely, remove from the heat and add the flour. Return to the heat and cook until the mixture rolls from the sides of the pan and there is a slight film of butter in the bottom of the pan. Add the eggs, one at a time, mixing well until each egg is completely absorbed, before adding the next egg. Add the flavoring of your choice.

Heat deep fat in a pan until it is moderately hot (the heat may be increased as the beignets brown). Drop small squares of the batter into the preheated fat. When the beignets finish turning over and are golden brown on both sides they are done. Drain them well on a towel, place in a warm dish and sprinkle with powdered sugar. Serve with custard sauce or fill with jam.

Cannoli

To make Cannoli, you must procure tubes of cane or tin that are about 6 inches long and an inch in diameter. The dough which will form the pastry shells is rolled into thin disks and then wrapped around the tubes to give the traditional scroll shape. The shells may be made in advance providing they are kept in an airtight container until the moment before they are to be filled and served. If the shells are filled too far in advance, they will become soggy and unmanageable.

Shells:
2 cups flour
1 tsp unsweetened powdered
 cocoa
¾ tsp powdered coffee
salt
1 tbsp granulated sugar
1 tbsp softened butter
4 oz white wine

Filling:
2 tbsps chopped candied orange
 and lemon peel, combined
½ lb ricotta cheese
¾ cup confectioners sugar
1 tbsp liqueur (your choice)
⅛ tsp vanilla extract
1 tsp powdered cocoa
3 oz semi-sweet chocolate bits
beaten egg white
candied cherries, halved, for decoration

Shells: Mix together 1¼ to 2 cups of flour, 1 tsp cocoa, the coffee powder, pinch of salt, and the granulated sugar. Make a well in the center and add the butter in small pieces. Knead the butter into the flour and add the wine to make a soft dough. Work the pastry for a few minutes and then form a ball. Wrap dough in a towel and let it rest for an hour.

Filling: In a bowl mix confectioners sugar, the liqueur, and the ricotta that has been pressed through a sieve. Mix until smooth and then add the chopped candied orange and lemon peels and the chocolate bits. Divide the filling in two parts and add a tsp of cocoa to one part and vanilla to the other. Refrigerate.

Grease pastry tubes. Roll dough very thin and cut out circles about 4″ in diameter. Stretch them with a rolling pin to make ovals. Place a tube lengthwise on each oval and roll the pastry around it, overlapping edges slightly. Stretch the dough a little at each end to widen openings. Brush beaten egg white over the edges so they will not open during cooking.

Place a deep-fryer, with an abundance of cooking oil, on a lively flame. When it is hot, not smoking, put the cannoli shells in, no more than two at a time, and fry until golden brown. Lift from the oil with care and drain on absorbent paper. When they have cooled somewhat, remove the tubes and allow shells to cool completely. The tubes may be used again, but be sure that they are completely cool.

Before serving: Fill the cooled shells with the cream: the vanilla half from one end and the chocolate half from the other. Place a halved cherry at each end. Arrange the cannoli on a serving plate and sprinkle with powdered sugar. Serve immediately.

Couronne de Pommes Amandine au Caramel
Apple Ring Amandine with Pralines

2 lbs apples, peeled and
 cored
½ cup almond powder
2 tbsps heavy cream
1 tsp corn starch diluted in
 2 cups milk

6 eggs, slightly beaten
1 tbsp rum, cognac or Calvados
 (optional)
2 tbsps praline powder
whipped cream or custard
 cream

Continued

Preheat oven to 375⁰.

Cut apples into quarters, then halve each quarter. Mix together sugar and almond powder. Add cream, corn starch and milk mixture, eggs and liqueur. Beat for a few minutes until smooth.

Grease a ring mold and coat with powdered praline. Pour in almond and egg mixture and stand apple sections on end all around mold. Bake in pre-heated oven for 35 to 40 minutes in a pan of water. Cool apple ring before unmolding, then fill center with sweetened whipped cream or custard cream.

Riz a l'Imperatrice   Empress Rice

This dessert doesn't look or taste like rice, but something truly royal! It is made with custard, glacéed fruit soaked in kirsch or rum, and whipped cream.

½ cup rice
1 cup thick custard:
   4 egg yolks, ½ cup sugar
   1 cup hot milk
½ pt (or 1¼ cups if you wish)
   heavy cream, whipped
currant jelly and more kirsch,
   or strawberries, or apricot
   glaze.

1 cup milk
4 to 6 oz glacéed fruit soaked
   in about ¼ cup kirsch or rum
1 or 1½ envs unflavored gelatin
vanilla to taste
more fruit to decorate

Rice: Cook 5 minutes in boiling water. Drain. Add hot milk (1 cup) and more later if needed. Cover and cook until soft. Check often. *Never add sugar to rice, or it will not cook.*

Custard: (No flour or cornstarch in this since rice is a starch.) Beat 4 yolks (3 if extra large) with ½ cup sugar. Add 1 cup hot milk slowly and pour in top of a double boiler. Cook, stirring, until it coats a spoon.

Dissolve gelatin in ¼ cup cold water in large mixing bowl. Pour the hot custard on the gelatin. Add the rice, and the fruit soaked with the kirsch. Mix well. Taste for sweetness and cool in refrigerator. Butter the mold and decorate the bottom with whole cherries and other colorful fruits.

Beat the whipped cream until fairly stiff. Add vanilla. Taste again for sweetness after you add the whipped cream to the rice mixture. The rice should be cold enough so the cream will not melt. Refrigerate 4 to 5 hours or overnight and unmold on platter.

Heat currant jelly (1½ cups) to melt it. Add liqueur, cool slightly, and pour around dessert or serve separately. Decorate with more fruit if desired.

Timbale Duchesse Anne

Jelly Roll

Jelly Roll:
4 eggs, separated
4 tbsps flour
4 tbsps sugar
vanilla or other flavoring
jelly or jam

Filling:
1 ½ cups apple sauce mixture
3 eggs
¹/₃ cup sugar
2 tbsps apricot jam
Calvados to taste
vanilla to taste

Apple Sauce:
3 lbs apples (Pippin)
juice of 1 lemon or orange
2 tbsps butter
Peel and coarsely chop apples.
 Cook slowly for 1 to 2 hours
 with lemon juice and butter.

Jelly Roll: Beat the sugar and yolks. Mix in half of the flour through a sifter. Beat egg whites with a dash of salt, and fold into sugar and yolks alternately with the rest of the flour. Spread batter on a well-greased cookie sheet or jelly roll pan. Bake 10 to 15 minutes at 350⁰ to 375⁰. Do not overbake or the cake will break when rolling. Frost with any kind of jam or jelly and roll up.
 Filling: Mix ingredients for filling together.
 To assemble: Slice the jelly roll and line a well-buttered 1-qt mold with the slices. Fill with filling mixture. Set mold in a pan of hot water and bake at 350⁰ for about 1 hour. Unmold dessert on a serving dish; serve with a sauce made of apricot (or other) jam mixed with a little heavy cream or sour cream.

Marquise Alice au Praline

Burnt Almond Pudding

4 eggs separated
2 pkgs lady fingers or stale
 cake
1 ½ cups whipped cream
sherry or cognac
currant jelly

4 tbsps sugar
1 ½ cups milk, warmed
1 envelope gelatin
For the praline: ½ cup sugar
 1 cup whole
 almonds with skins

Praline: Put the sugar and almonds with a little water in a pan over a high fire until they carmelize. Then drop this mixture onto an oiled marble slab, or any kind of hard surface. When cold, pound it, reducing it to a coarse pulp. Save a little of the pulp to spread on the side of the finished pudding.
 Pudding: Work sugar and yolks together. Add hot milk and place in a double boiler, and stir until it becomes creamy. Dissolve one envelope of gelatin in a little cold water. Pour hot mixture over the gelatin and stir until completely melted. Let it cool a little and then add one cup of whipped cream and the egg whites beaten stiff. Add praline and mix well. Line a mold with

Continued

lady fingers or stale cake and sprinkle with a little sherry or cognac. Pour some of the pudding over the cake, then add another layer of cake. Repeat layers until the mold is full, finishing with a layer of pudding. Chill well and unmold and cover the whole pudding with the rest of the whipped cream. Fill a paper tube with currant jelly and draw thin parallel lines across the whipped cream. With a knife, run lightly across these lines, first in one direction and then in the other. This will make a zig-zag design.

Pommes en Croûte   Apples in a Crust

1 recipe puff pastry or   1 cup sugar
   pâte brissé   1 egg yolk
6 good-sized apples   currant jelly
6 walnut halves   1 cup heavy cream, whipped
½ cup butter plus 2 tbsps

   Peel and core apples. Roll out pastry, cut into 6 large squares, and set an apple on each. Poke a walnut into each hollow and top with butter and sugar.
   Wrap pastry around apples, sealing edges with a little water. Brush with beaten egg yolk. Bake in a preheated 375° oven for 30 minutes or until brown. Serve warm with currant jelly and whipped cream.

Melons Meringues

2 small cantaloupes   2 cups fruit in season,
   (½ melon per person)   marinated in kirsch, Curaçao,
2 egg whites   or brandy. (peaches, strawberries,
1 tbsp vanilla   apricots, currants, blackberries,
²/₃ cup sugar (¹/₃ cup   pineapple, etc.)
   sugar per egg white)

   Cut melons crosswise — scallop edge if desired. Remove a bit of the melon flesh to enlarge the cavity. Add the melon flesh to the marinating fruit. Add a little more liqueur to marinating fruit close to serving time. Fill melon cavities with fruit.
   In the top of a double-boiler put the sugar and egg whites. Beat with an electric mixer, preferably over boiling water — keep beating well, reaching around bottom of pan to prevent whites from cooking. Whites will get thick and glossy. Continue beating until they no longer drip from beaters. This takes about 4 to 5 minutes. Add vanilla. Meringue can be made in advance. Keep covered to prevent a crust from forming.
   Top melons with meringue. Put into preheated 550° oven until tops are golden.

Poires au Sabayon

Pears with Sabayon

4 servings

4 pears, poached
3 to 4 egg yolks

$^1/_3$ cup sherry or white wine
4 tbsps sugar

Prepare the poached pears (see glossary).

Mix together the egg yolks, wine or sherry, and the sugar in the top of a double boiler over hot water. Beat until it becomes thick and forms a ribbon when dropped from the beater.

Arrange the poached pears in a deep dish and pour the sabayon over them. Serve immediately.

Sabayon Froid

Cold Sabayon

8 egg yolks
$^3/_4$ to 1 cup sugar

1 cup cream sherry
or French sauterne

Put the egg yolks, sugar and sherry in a large bowl over hot water on the stove. Beat for 5 to 7 minutes with an electric mixer. Transfer the bowl to a large bowl of ice and continue to beat until the mixture is cool. Spoon it into glasses, such as sherry or champagne glasses. Serve.

Ananas

Pineapple Filled with Fresh Fruit Gelatin

1 large pineapple, halved
1 tbsp gelatin
kirsch
fresh berries dipped in
   powdered sugar for garnish

½ cup heavy cream, whipped
crushed raspberries or strawberries
1 tsp vanilla
2 tbsps sugar
Syrup: $^1/_3$ cup water
       ½ cup sugar

Halve the pineapple and carefully scoop out the flesh. Slice and marinate in kirsch. Scrape out the rest of the pulp and set aside. Make a syrup by combining the sugar and water and heat over medium heat. Cook until it thickens, about 10 minutes. Add pulp and cook to reduce slightly. Soften gelatin in a little cold water and pour the hot syrup over. Stir to dissolve the gelatin. Cool. Add the crushed berries — the amount will depend on how deep a color is desired.

Whip the cream with the sugar, adding more if necessary. Stir in the vanilla. Combine the cream and the pulp mixture. Fill the pineapple shells. If desired, dip the fresh berries into powdered sugar and place on top of the halves.

Pêches Regane

Kirsch Jelly:
1½ cups water
1 cup sugar
1 tbsp unflavored gelatin
¾ cup kirsch

poached peach halves,
     1 per serving
¾ cup heavy cream,
     whipped with 2 tbsps sugar
wild strawberries or quartered
     berries for garnish
buttered muffin tins or
     other individual deep molds

Peaches with Kirsch Jelly

Pâte Frolle:
1¾ cups flour
8 tbsps butter, melted and cooled
1 cup ground almonds
1 cup sugar
2 large eggs
1 tbsp vanilla
½ tsp almond extract
dash of salt
zest of 1 lemon

Prepare kirsch jelly by boiling the sugar and water together for 5 minutes. Remove from heat. Soften the gelatin in cold water and stir into the syrup. Stir in the kirsch and refrigerate. This will yield a little over 2 cups of jelly.

Prepare Pâte Frolle by combining all ingredients and mixing thoroughly. Cool to facilitate rolling. Roll and cut circles to fit molds. Press into molds, trimming excess, and place a small piece of tin foil against the dough as this will prevent shrinkage during baking. Bake in a 375⁰ oven for 12 to 15 minutes.

To assemble: When the pastry shells have cooled, fill partially with the jelly. If the jelly has completely jelled, it can be chopped before adding. Place the peach halves on top. Using a pastry bag, pipe a circle of whipped cream around the edge and a star on top. Set 4 to 5 berries into the whipped cream and one on top.

Charlotte aux Goyats

1 env gelatine
½ cup cold water
4 eggs
⅓ cup sugar
1 cup milk
1 tsp vanilla

Guava Charlotte

1 lb guavas
juice of 1 lemon
1 pkg lady fingers
½ pt whipping cream
glacé cherries

Soak the gelatin in a little cold water to soften. Beat the eggs and the sugar. Warm the milk to the boiling point in a double boiler and add to the eggs and sugar. Return the mixture to the double boiler and stir until the cream coats a spoon. Add the melted gelatin and let the custard cool until it becomes syrupy. Add the vanilla.

Cook the guavas in a small amount of water and the juice of one lemon. Strain and purée in the blender and add to the cooled custard.

Grease a mold and line it with lady fingers.

Whip the cream and add half of it to the guava mixture. Pour it into the mold and refrigerate for at least 4 hours. To unmold, dip in hot water and reverse on a serving platter. Decorate with the remaining whipped cream and glacé cherries.

Champagne Sherbet

1 cup water
juice of 2 oranges
juice of 1 lemon

3 cups sugar
rind of 1 orange, grated
half-bottle champagne,
    or split

Combine sugar and water. Over medium heat cook until syrup reaches "soft-ball" stage. Bring champagne to a boil to remove the alcohol as alcohol will keep the sherbet from freezing. Add juice of lemon and oranges, the orange rind, and the syrup to the champagne. If using an ice cream maker follow the manufacturer's instructions. Otherwise, place in the freezer and mix frequently until mixture has frozen.

Glacé aux Mures   Blackberry Ice Cream

2 cups blackberries
1 cup sugar
½ cup water

juice of 1 lemon
½ pt whipping cream

Cook the blackberries, sugar, water, and lemon juice for 5 minutes. Strain the juice and cook until it is reduced to 1½ cups. Let it cool. Whip the cream and add it to the juice. Churn the mixture in an ice cream freezer. Set it in a mold and keep in the freezer until ready to serve.

MENUS

Menus

Caprices de Volaille*	Chicken in Pastry*
Souffle au Fromage et aux*	Cheese Souffle with Herbs*
Herbes du Jardin	Green Salad
Salade Verte	Strawberry Tartlets
Tartelets aux Fraises	

Allumettes a la Reine (bouchees)*	Queen's Match Sticks*
Potage Printanier	Consomme with Vegetables
Filets de Sole Marguery*	Filets of Sole with Shrimp and Mussels*
Escalopes de Veau aux Epinards	Veal Scallops and Spinach
Pommes de Terre Macaire*	Sautéed Baked Potatoes*
Auguste Escoffier	Creamed Spinach and Lettuce
Epinards a la Laitue	Jello Pie
Le Multicolore	

Soupe a la Choucroute	Fresh Sauerkraut Soup
Escalopes de Veau a L'Alsatienne*	Alsatian Scaloppine*
Les Carres de Semoule	Cream of Wheat Cakes
Les Navets Aigres	Turnips in Sour Cream
Gateau Alsacien*	Alsatian Coffee Cake*
Compote de Fruit	Stewed Fruits

Canapés Jeannette	Liver Paste Canapés
Potage Crème Chàtelaine*	Cream of Artichoke Soup*
Filets de Merlans Colbert	Filets of Whiting Colbert
Gigot au Gingembre*	Ginger Leg of Lamb*
Haricots Verts Panachés	Mixed Green and Dried Beans
Pots-De-Crème Au Café*	Coffee Custard Cups*

Artichauts Pompadour
Potage Rouennais (Normandie)
Poulet Champenoise*
Pommes de Terre Dauphine*
Timbles D'Epinards*
Tarte Charles (Ile-de-France)*

Artichoke Hearts Pompadour
Lamb and Vegetable Soup
Chicken Champenoise*
Potatoes Dauphine*
Spinach Timbales*
Apple Tart Charles*

Paupiettes d'Anchois Batelière
Potage Vichyssoise Joséphine*
Tomates Gabrielle
Emincé de Boeuf Paloise
Pommes de Terre Berrichonne
Chou-Fleur Polonaise
Marquise Alice au Praline*

Anchovy Scrolls with Puff Paste
Vichyssoise Joséphine*
Stuffed Tomatoes with Avocado
and Tuna
Strips of Beef with Mushrooms
and Wine
Potatoes with Broth, Onions
and Bacon
Cauliflower with Bread Crumb Sauce
Burnt Almond Pudding*

Canapés d'Eglefin Fumé*
Potage à l'Oseille
Ris de Veau, Issigny*
Epinard Beaurivage
Croutes aux Peches
Sauce Sabayon*

Smoked Haddock Canapes*
Cream of Sorrel Soup
Sweet Breads with Cream*
Spinach and Noodles
Peaches on Toast
Sabayon Sauce*

Canapés Domino
Pistou (Provence)*
Boeuf Mode en Gelee*
Pommes de Terre en Purée
Chou de Bruxelle Et Concomeres
Beignets de Pommes

Domino Canapés
Pistou Soup*
Beef a la Mode in Jelly*
Mashed Potatoes
Brussel Sprouts and Cucumbers
Apple Fritters

Croûtes au Pot*
Filets de Sole Chauchat*
Tournedos Bourguignon*
Laitues Braisées au Madère
Gateau de Riz au Caramel

Beef Broth with Vegetables
and Toasted Bread*
Fillets of Sole with Potatoes
and Béchamel Sauce*
Filet or Top Sirloin Rounds
with Burgundy*
Braised Lettuce Madeira
Rice Cake with Caramel

Talmousses aux Epinards*
Potage a la Reine
Boeuf Bourguignon Josephine*
Terrine de Courgettes
Pommes de Terre Badoise
Soufflé Peter Swain

Spinach in Crust*
Queen Potage
Beef Stew Josephine*
Zucchini Casserole
Mashed Potato with Egg
Chocolate Soufflé Peter Swain

CULINARY GLOSSARY

Culinary Glossary

Aioli:
Sauce for vegetables made of six to seven cloves of garlic, pounded with a mortar and pestle, and added to one cup of mayonnaise, homemade or commercial.

Anglaise:
Any preparation cooked mostly in water or white stock. Also, breadcrumbs coated with an oil, egg and milk mixture.

Amalgamer:
To amalgamate or mix thoroughly without stirring too vigorously.

Arroser:
To baste a roast or other foods with butter, broth, or the fat and juices of the roast.

Aromatic Herbs:
Strong seasoning made by chopping and combining any or all of the following: oregano, winter savory, marjoram, sage, chives.

Baba:
Cake made of raised dough, with or without raisins and soaked in rum or kirsch syrup after baking.

Bain-marie:
A vessel of hot water in which sauces and dishes can be set to stay hot, usually kept on top of the stove.

Ballotine:
Boned, stuffed and rolled meat, fowl, or fish molded into a cylinder shape and wrapped in cheese cloth or skin. Normally served hot as a first course.

Barder:
Wrapping a piece of meat, poultry, game or fish with strips of fresh or salted pork fat known as fat back, in preparation for braising.

Bardes:
Slices of fat back used for barding meat, poultry, game.

Baveuse:
Term for describing the desired consistency of a properly made omelet; it means "mellow" or "moist."

Béchamel:
Fundamental sauce made of butter, flour and egg yolk added to a cream base.

Beignets:
Fritters, or any food dipped in batter and deep fat fried.

Beurre manié:
Thickening agent for sauces made of equal parts flour and butter, mixed into a paste and brought to the boiling point.

Binding:
Process of thickening a sauce that is too thin.

Blanc:
A mixture of flour and water in which various vegetables and meats can be cooked to keep them white (cauliflower, sweetbreads, etc).

Blanch:
To submerge any ingredient in boiling salted water for varying amounts of time in order to cook or harden it.

Blondir:
To brown very lightly in butter, oil or fat; also, to cook flour and butter together to form a light roux.

Bouilli:
Boiled beef.

Bouillie:
Pulp or gruel.

Bouillir:
To boil rapidly in salted water.

Bordure:
Dishes that are served in a ring or crown-shaped mold. The mold may be made of Duchesse potatoes, rice, semolina, etc. for hot dishes; jelly, custards, cream, riz a l'emperatrice, etc., for cold or sweet dishes.

Bouchées:
Small patty shells or cream puffs, filled, and served as hors d'oeuvres, before or after the soup course.

Bouquet garni:
A packet of herbs tied together and added to the dish while cooking, usually made of thyme, bay leaf, and parsley. Amount should be judged sparingly, but according to the size of the dish being prepared. For some dishes, bouquets are made of highly scented herbs, such as basil, celery, tarragon, rosemary, sage, etc. The bouquet is removed from the sauce or dish before serving.

Canapés:
Toasted or fried bread cut into round, rectangular or other shapes and spread with various mixtures. Served as appetizers or luncheon entrees.

Cassoulet:
A casserole composed of beans and meat.

Chiffonade:
Chopped lettuce, sorrel, spinach and other herbs added to soups at the last minute as a garnish.

Caul:
Or crepine is the membrane enclosing the belly of the pig. It is boiled and used to line and cover pâté, or to wrap meats for cooking. Strips of fresh pork fat can be used as a substitute.

Chapeler:
Preparation of breadcrumbs from bread that has been dried, crushed with a rolling pin or bottle, and passed through a metal sieve.

Chevaler:
The symmetrical arrangement of various ingredients of a dish, placed to overlap one another.

Coagulate:
To thicken or congeal fats and jellies.

Corder:
An excess of water mixed into pastry dough, causing it to bake leather-hard, and be unpalatable.

Cornichons:
Small sour pickles.

Court bouillon:
A cooking liquid made by simmering together vegetables, wine, and stock.

Creme a l'Anglaise:
A custard cream made of egg yolks, sugar, milk or cream thickened in a double boiler.

Crème Frâiche:
Stir 2 tbsps sour cream or buttermilk into 1 cup whipping cream. Let stand at room temperature for 24 hours. If very warm, refrigerate after 12 hours.

Crepine:
Same as caul.

Croustades:
Thick slices of bread, hollowed out and toasted in the oven until dried out and browned.

Croutons:
Dried-out bread that is toasted or fried and then cut into ¼ to ½" cubes; or can be cut to the shape of the meat being prepared, to be used as a foundation for the dish, as in tournedos.

Deglacer (or de-glaze):
A technical term for the dilution of the concentrated juice in a pan in which meat, poultry, game or fish has been roasted, braised or fried. Wine, soup stock or cream can be used for this purpose.

Degorger:
To soak food for any length of time in cold water to free it from any impurities (calves' head, veal sweetbreads, brains, etc.)

Demi feuilletée:
See Pâté.

Demi-glacé:
A basic brown sauce.

Duxelle:
A mixture of mushrooms with onion, shallots and nutmeg.

Duchess potatoes:
Mashed potatoes with egg yolk added, used as a decorative border and garnish for meat and fish dishes.

Emince:
A dish made with left-over roast or braised meat. The meat is thinly sliced and placed in a casserole and covered with a sauce (Bordelaise, mushroom, etc.).

Emincer:
Meaning to slice very finely meats, vegetables, fruits.

Entrée:
Literally "beginning," but in the culinary sense it *does not* refer to the first course. The entrée in a full French menu follows the relève, or intermediate course, coming as the third course in the meal.

Etuver:
To cook food in a covered pan without moistening. This method of cooking is suitable for all kinds of meat, poultry, vegetables, and fruit. Butter, fat or oil is added.

Farci:
Preparation of veal, chicken or any fowl by stuffing the breast and then roasting, frying or poaching the meat. Any kind of forcemeat can be used for stuffing.

Fat back, or pork fat:
Fat layer next to the skin from the back of a pig. Cut into strips; it is used to line pâtés or wrap meat for cooking.

Fine herbs:
The combination of these herbs is recommended for salads, omelets, soups, vegetables, chicken and fish: parsley, chervil, tarragon, chives, fennel, basil, sorrel, spinach, dill, savory.

Fleurons:
Small crescent-shaped decorations made from any kind of pastry dough or toast, served as a garnish for meat or fish.

Fond blanc:
White stock.

Fond brun:
Brown stock.

Forcemeat or stuffing (farces):

A mixture of ingredients, minced and seasoned and used in pâtès, gallantine, eggs, fish, poultry, meat and vegetables.

Fraises:

Strawberries.

Fricassee:

Preparation of poultry in a white sauce.

Fumet:

Liquid used to flavor or give body to stocks and sauces. Fumets are prepared by boiling foodstuffs in wine or stock made from meat or fish.

Gallantine:

A dish made from boned poultry or meat, stuffed and then pressed into a shape and poached in a gelatin stock. Served cold.

Garbure:

Substantial soup made with vegetables, pork and beef with cabbage added one half hour before serving.

Garnish:

Trimming added to a dish or placed around it; or served separately to accompany it. It should always blend with the flavor of the basic dish. Garnishes are classified as simple or composite.

Glacage:

There is no single English equivalent for this term. It is used to refer to several quite distinct operations. Literally glacer means to freeze a liquid until it turns to ice (ice cream), but it can also refer to culinary operations carried out in an excessively hot oven. Meat is said to be browned if served hot, and glazed (with jelly) if served cold.

Glacage can refer to covering fish, eggs, etc., with a white sauce.

Glacage can mean sprinkling sweets or vegetables (carrots, turnips, onions) with confectioners sugar and subjecting them to high heat.

Glacage: term for the icing of cakes.

Glace de viande:

Concentrated beef extract.

Gratin:

The thin crust formed on the surface of certain dishes when browned in the oven or broiler.

Grenadins:

Slices of filet (sirloin) of veal, shaped round (tournedos) or rectangular, larded with bacon and braised.

Hors d'oeuvre:

There are two main types of hors d'oeuvre: cold and hot. They are sometimes called entrées volantes, or light entrées; generally served after the soup, but can precede it as well.

Inciser:
Making light incisions with a very sharp knife in the skin of fish to be grilled or fried.

Isigny:
A small town in Calvados, France where some of the best butter in France is made.

Jardiniere:
A garnish made of fresh vegetables.

Jus:
In French, it has a wider connotation than in English: Juice pressed from an animal or vegetable; gravy made by diluting the juices of the roasting; brown stock of veal, especially that which is clear or thickened and used as gravy.

Julienne:
Any foodstuffs coarsely or finely shredded.

Kirsch:
Cherry flavored liqueur used in cooking.

Larding:
Strips of fat threaded through cuts of meat by means of a larding needle.

Lardons:
Strips of fresh bacon or fat used in larding.

Liaison:
Thickening process of adding egg yolk and cream or broth to a sauce or liquid, removed from the heat. Arrowroot or cornstarch used as a liaison must be diluted first in a little cream or broth.

Madrilene:
A clear soup served hot or cold, flavored with tomato sauce.

Marinade:
A seasoned liquid, cooked or uncooked, in which foodstuffs (notably meat and fish) are steeped for a length of time.

Marmite:
A metal or earthenware covered pot, used for bisques and garbure and for the famous French pot-au-feu.

Mirepoix:
Sauteed mixture of celery, carrot and onion.

Mets:
A term for any food prepared for the table.

Mignonette:
Coarse ground pepper.

Mille feuille:
A pastry of a "thousand leaves", in America, a "Napoleon."

Napper:
To cover meat, poultry or fish all at once with a thick Velouté or other sauce.

Panade:
Cooked mixture of butter, flour and water used as a thickener. Adding whole eggs makes it Pâte à choux.

Panure:
To coat with breadcrumbs, first coating with melted butter or beaten eggs.

Parisian Seasoning:
See Section on Seasonings.

Parmentier:
Method of preparing various dishes which always includes potatoes in one form or another.

Pâte:
Basic dough, includes pâte feuilletage, pâte brisée, bread dough, batters and sweet pastes.

Pâte demi-feuilletée:
Rises half as high as regular puff paste. Using puff paste recipe, use 6 ounces butter and 2 ounces water. Give only 3 to 4 turns, and continue as for puff pastry.

Pâté:
A meat "paste."

Pâté en croute:
Pâté baked in a pastry crust.

Pâté galantine:
Pâté baked as stuffing inside turkey or chicken.

Pâté Terrine:
Pâté served in a baking dish.

Paupiettes:
Thin slices of beef or veal, stuffed and rolled, wrapped in slices of bacon and simmered in very little liquid.

Persillade:
Chopped parsley, often mixed with chopped garlic; also refers to leftover meat that is fried in butter.

Pesto:
A pounding of garlic, basil and parmesan cheese with addition of olive oil. A soup base.

Petits fours:
Many kinds of small fancy cakes.

Pigeon:
Squab.

Poach:
To cook meat, poultry, fish, etc., in a clear, spiced and flavored stock.

Pommes de terre:
Potatoes.

Profiterolles:
Small cream puffs, which may be filled with ice cream, creme patissiere or other fillings.

Purée:
Food that is mashed and put through a sieve.

Quenelles:
Dumpling made with fish or forcemeat.

Raidir:
To sear a foodstuff quickly in very hot butter or fat.

Reduction:
To decrease the volume of a liquid by evaporation (in sauce making).

Remonter:
Addition of a spice to a sauce or alcohol to wine to strengthen or heighten its taste.

Rouleau:
Preparation that is rolled into shape; usually filled with another mixture, such as cheese roll or jelly roll.

Roux:
Cooked mixture of flour and butter.

Salpiçon:
Several ingredients finely diced and mixed together, such as ham, mushrooms, etc.

Sauté:
To cook over a high fire in butter, oil or fat, stirring frequently.

Soupçon:
A little bit; a dash.

Stock:
Liquid obtained from cooking meat, bones and vegetables together. If it is clarified, it becomes consommé.

Terrine:
Baking dish, oval or rectangular, particularly for pâté.

Timbale:
A custard containing cooked vegetables and meat.

Tomber:
This is an old French cooking term (meaning literally "to fall") to describe method of cooking meat without any other liquid in the pan than that produced by the meat itself. The moisture created in the cooking must reduce to a syrupy consistency. *Tomber a glace* means to add a small amount of liquid, and then boil down completely.

Travailler:
To beat a sauce, dough, or mixture.

Trognon:
Edible heart of a vegetable or fruit.

Truffle:
A fungus for garnish and stuffings. In France, the province of Perigord is famous for truffles.

Velouté:
A fundamental sauce made of butter, flour and egg yolk added to broth.

Vinaigrette:
Sauce or marinade of oil and vinegar; French dressing.

Zest:
Orange or lemon peel, made with a utensil called a *zesteur*.

INDEX

Index